Small Business Management

Essential Ingredients for Success

MEIR LIRAZ

Published by BizMove
www.bizmove.com

Copyright © 2017 Meir Liraz

All rights reserved.

ISBN: 1974123391
ISBN-13: 978-1974123391

Table of Contents

1	How to Make Your Business More Profitable	5
2	Essential Ingredients for Your Marketing Success	19
3	Twenty Seven Tips to Increase the Effectiveness of Your Delegation	33
4	How to Reach Your Goals Faster	37
5	How to Deal with Changes in The Market	43
6	How to Build a Winning Team	47
7	How to Make a Good First Impression	51
8	How to Manage Your Business Successfully	56
9	Financial Management Essentials	72
10	Developing a Marketing Plan	86
11	Basics of Business Management	100
12	Achieving Customer Satisfaction and Loyalty	121
13	Five Special Free Bonuses (download links are provided)	137

MEIR LIRAZ

1. How to Make Your Business More Profitable

Making a profit is the most important - some might say the only - objective of a business. Profit measures success. It can be defined simply: Revenues - Expenses = Profit. So, to increase profits you must raise revenues, lower expenses, or both. To make improvements you must know what's really going on financially at all times. You have to watch every financial event without any kind of optimistic filter.

This chapter is a series of questions with comments to help you analyze your profits, their sufficiency and trend, the contribution of each of your product lines or services to them, and to help you determine if you have the kind of record system you need. The questions and comments are not meant to be definitive presentations on the subjects. They are meant to point to areas where further study might be - well - profitable.

Are You making A Profit?

Analysis of Revenues and Expenses

Since profit is revenues less expenses, to determine what your profit is you must first identify all revenues and expenses for the period under study.

1. Have you chosen an appropriate period for profit determination?

For accounting purposes firms generally use a twelve month period, such as January 1 to December 31 or July 1 to June 30. The accounting year you select doesn't have to be a calendar year (January to December); a seasonal business, for example, might close its year after the end of the season. The selection depends upon the nature of your business, your personal preference, or possible tax considerations.

2. Have you determined your total revenues for the accounting period?

In order to answer this question, consider the following questions:

What is the amount of gross revenue from sales of your goods or service? (Gross Sales)

What is the amount of goods returned by your customers and credited? (Returns and Rejects)

What is the amount of discounts given to your customers and employees? (Discounts)

What is the amount of net sales from goods and services? (Net Sales = Gross Sales - Returns and Rejects + Discounts))

What is the amount of income from other sources, such as interest on bank deposits, dividends from securities, rent on property leased to others? (Non-operating Income)

What is the amount of total revenue? (Total Revenue =

Net Sales + Non-operating Income)

3. Do you know what your total expenses are?

Expenses are the cost of goods sold and services used in the process of selling goods or services. Some common expenses for all businesses are:

Cost of goods sold (Cost of Goods Sold = Beginning Inventory + Purchases - Ending Inventory)

Wages and salaries (Don't forget to include your own- at the actual rate - you'd have to pay someone else to do your job.)

Rent

Utilities (electricity, gas telephone, water, etc.)

Delivery expenses

Insurance

Advertising and promotional costs

Maintenance and upkeep

Depreciation (Here you need to make sure your depreciation policies are realistic and that all depreciable items are included)

Taxes and licenses

Interest

Bad debts

Professional assistance (accountant, attorney, etc.)

There are of course, many other types of expenses, but the point is that every expense must be recorded and deducted from your revenues before you know what your profit is. Understanding your expenses is the first step toward controlling them and increasing your profit.

Financial Ratios

A financial ratio is an expression on the relationship between two items selected from the income statement or the balance sheet. Ratio analysis helps you evaluate the weak and strong points in your financial and managerial performance.

4. Do you know your current ratio?

The current ratio (current assets divided by current debts) is a measure of the cash or near cash position (liquidity) of the firm. It tells you if you have enough cash to pay your firm's current creditors. The higher the ratio, the more liquid the firm's position is and, hence, the higher the credibility of the firm. Cash, receivables, marketable securities, and inventory are current assets. Naturally you need to be realistic in valuing receivable and inventory for a true picture of your liquidity, since some debts may be uncollectable and some stock obsolete. Current liabilities are those which must be paid in one year.

5. Do you know your quick ratio?

Quick assets are current assets minus inventory. The quick

ratio (or acid-test ratio) is found by dividing quick assets by current liabilities. The purpose, again, is to test the firm's ability to meet its current obligations. This test doesn't include inventory to make it a stiffer test of the company's liquidity. It tells you if the business could meet its current obligations with quickly convertible assets should sales revenue suddenly cease.

6. Do you know your total debt to net worth ratio?

This ratio (the result of total debt divided by net worth then multiplied by 100) is a measure of how company can meet its total obligation from equity. The lower the ratio, the higher the proportion of equity relative to debt and the better the firm's credit rating will be.

7. Do you know your average collection period?

You find this ratio by dividing accounts receivable by daily credit sales. (Daily credit sales = annual credit sales divided by 360.) This ratio tells you the length of time it takes the firm to get its cash after making a sale on credit. The shorter this period the quicker the cash flow is. A longer than normal period may mean overdue and un-collectible bills. If you extend credit for a specific period (say, 30 days), this ratio should be very close to the same number of day. If it's much longer than the established period, you may need to alter your credit policies. It's wise to develop an aging schedule to gauge the trend of collections (without adequate financing charges) hurt your profit, since you could be doing something much more useful with your money, such as taking advantage of discounts on your own payables.

8. Do you know your ratio of net sales to total assets?

This ratio (net sales divided by total assets) measures the efficiency with which you are using your assets. A higher than normal ratio indicates that the firm is able to generate sales from its assets faster (and better) than the average concern.

9. Do you know your operating profit to net sales ratio?

This ratio (the result of dividing operating profit by net sales and multiplying by 100) is most often used to determine the profit position relative to sales. A higher than normal ratio indicates that your sales are good, that your expenses are low, or both. Interest income and interest expense should not be included in calculating this ratio.

10. Do you know your net profit to total assets ratio?

This ratio (found by multiplying by 100 the result of dividing net profit by total assets) is often called return on investment or ROI. It focuses on the profitability of the overall operation of the firm. Thus, it allows management to measure the effects of its policies on the firm's profitability. The ROI is the single most important measure of a firm's financial position. You might say it's the bottom line for the bottom line.

11. Do you know your net profit to net worth ratio?

This ratio is found by dividing net profit by net worth and multiplying the result by 100. It provides information on the productivity of the resources the owners have committed to the firm's operations.

All ratios measuring profitability can be computed either before or after taxes, depending on the purpose of the computations. Ratios have limitations. Since the information used to derive ratios is itself based on accounting rules and personal judgments, as well as facts, the ratios cannot be considered absolute indicators of a firm's financial position. Ratios are only one means of assessing the performance of the firm and must be considered in perspective with many other measures. They should be used as a point of departure for further analysis and not as an end in themselves.

Sufficiency Of Profit

The following questions are designed to help you measure the adequacy of the profit your firm is making. Making a profit is only the first step; making enough profit to survive and grow is really what business is all about.

12. Have you compared your profit with your profit goals?

13. Is it possible your goals are too high or too low?

14. Have you compared your present profits (absolute and ratios) with the profits made in the last one to three years?

15. Have you compared your profits (absolute and ratios) with profits made by similar firms in your line?

A number of organizations publish financial ratios for various businesses, among them Dun & Bradstreet. Robert Morris Associates, the Accounting Corporation of America, NCR Corporation, and the Bank of America. Your own trade association may also publish such studies. Remember, these published ratios are only averages. You probably want to be better than average.

Trend Of Profit

16. Have you analyzed the direction your profits have been taking?

The preceding analysis, with all their merits, report on a firm only at a single time in the past. It is not possible to use these isolated moments to indicate the trend of your firm's performance. To do a trend analysis performance indicators (absolute amounts or ratios) should be computed for several time periods (yearly for several years, for example) and the results laid out in columns side by side for easy comparison. You can then evaluate your performance, see the direction it's taking, and make initial forecasts of where it will go.

17. Does your firm sell more than one major product line or provide several distinct services?

If it does, a separate profit and ratio analysis of each should be made:

To show the relative contribution by each product line or service;

To show the relative burden of expenses by each product or service;

To show which items are most profitable, which are less so, and which are losing money; and to show which are slow and fast moving.

Mix Of Profit

The profit analysis of each major item help you find out the strong and weak areas of your operations. They can help you to make profit-increasing decisions to drop a product line or service or to place particular emphasis behind one or another.

Records

Good records are essential. Without them a firm doesn't know where it's been, where it is, or where it's heading. Keeping records that are accurate, up-to-date, and easy to use is one of the most important functions of the owner-manager, his or her staff, and his or her outside counselors (lawyer, accountant, banker).

Basic Records

18. Do you have a general journal and/or special journals, such as one for cash receipts and disbursements?

A general journal is the basic record of the firm. Every monetary event in the life of the firm is entered in the general journal or in one of the special journals.

19. Do you prepare a sales report or analysis?

(a) Do you have sales goals by product, department, and accounting period (month, quarter, year)?

(b) Are your goals reasonable?

(c) Are you meeting your goals?

If you aren't meeting your goals, try to list the likely reasons on a sheet of paper. Such a study might include areas such as general business climate, competition, pricing, advertising, sales promotion, credit policies, and the like. Once you've identified the apparent causes you can take steps to increase sales (and profits).

Buying and Inventory System

20. Do you have a buying and inventory system?

The buying and inventory systems are two critical areas of a firm's operation that can affect profitability.

21. Do you keep records on the quality, service, price, and promptness of delivery of your sources of supply?

22. Have you analyzed the advantages and disadvantages of:

(a) Buying from several suppliers,

(b) Buying from a minimum number of suppliers?

23. Have you analyzed the advantages and disadvantages of buying through cooperatives or other systems?

24. Do you know:

(a) How long it usually takes to receive each order?

(b) How much inventory cushion (usually called safety stock) to have so you can maintain normal sales while you wait for the order to arrive?

25. Have you ever suffered because you were out of stock?

26. Do you know the optimum order quantity for each item you need?

27. Do you (or can you) take advantage of quantity discounts for large size single purchases?

28. Do you know your costs of ordering inventory and carrying inventory?

The more frequently you buy (smaller quantities per order), the higher your average ordering costs (clerical costs, postage, telephone costs etc.) will be, and the lower the average carrying costs (storage, loss through pilferage, obsolescence, etc.) will be. On the other hand, the larger the quantity per order, the lower the average ordering cost and the higher the carrying costs. A balance should be struck so that the minimum cost overall for ordering and carrying inventory can be achieved.

29. Do you keep records of inventory for each item?

These records should be kept current by making entries whenever items are added to or removed from inventory. Simple records on 3 x 5 or 5 x 7 cards can be used with each item being listed on a separate card. Proper records will show for each item: quantity in stock, quantity on order, date of order, slow or fast seller, and valuations (which are important for taxes and your own analyses.)

Other Financial Records

30. Do you have an accounts payable ledger?

This ledger will show what, whom, and why you owe. Such records should help you make your payments on schedule. Any expense not paid on time could adversely affect your credit, but even more importantly such records should help you take advantage of discounts which can help boost your profits.

31. Do you have an accounts receivable ledger?

This ledger will show who owes money to your firm. It shows how much is owed, how long it has been outstanding and why the money is owed. Overdue accounts could indicate that your credit granting policy needs to be reviewed and that you may not be getting the cash into the firm quickly enough to pay your own bills at the optimum time.

32. Do you have a cash receipts journal?

This journal records the cash received by source, day, and amount.

33. Do you have a cash payments journal?

This journal will be similar to the cash receipts journal but will show cash paid out instead of cash received. The two cash journals can be combined, if convenient.

34. Do you prepare an income (profit and loss or P&L) statement and a balance sheet?

These are statements about the condition of your firm at a specific time and show the income, expenses, assets, and liabilities of the firm. They are absolutely essential.

35. Do you prepare a budget?

You could think of a budget as a "record in advance," projecting "future" inflows and outflows for your business. A budget is usually prepared for a single year, generally to correspond with the accounting year. It is then, however broken down into quarterly and monthly projections.

There are different kinds of budget: cash, production, sales, etc. A cash budget, for example, will show the estimate of sales and expenses for a particular period of time. The cash budget forces the firm to think ahead by estimating its income and expenses. Once reasonable projections are made for every important product line or department, the owner-manager has set targets for employees to meet for sales and expenses. You must plan to assure a profit. And you must prepare a budget to plan.

2. Essential Ingredients for Your Marketing Success

One great need of small business managers is to understand and develop marketing programs for their products and services. Long term small business success depends on the ability to maintain a strong body of satisfied customers while continually increasing this body with new customers. Modern marketing programs build around the marketing concept, which directs managers to focus their efforts on identifying, satisfying, and following up the customer's needs - all at a profit.

THE MARKETING CONCEPT

The marketing concept rests on the importance of customers to a firm. All company policies and activities should be aimed at satisfying customer needs while obtaining a profitable rather than maximum sales volume.

To use the marketing concept, a small business should:

* Determine the needs of their customers (marketing research).

* Develop their competitive advantages (market strategy).

* Select specific markets to serve (target marketing).

* Determine how to satisfy those needs (marketing mix).

* Analyze how well they've served their customers, and then return to step 1 (marketing performance).

MARKET RESEARCH

The aim of market research is to find out who the customers are, what the customers want, where and when they want it. This research can also expose problems in the current product or service, and find areas for expansion of current services to fill customer demand. Market research should also encompass identifying trends that may affect sales and profit levels.

Market research should give you more information, however, than just who your customers are. Use this information to determine matters such as your market share, the effectiveness of your advertising and promotions, and the response to new product developments that you have introduced into the market.

For once, small business holds an edge. While larger companies hire professionals to do their research, small business managers are close to their customers. They can learn much more quickly the likes and dislikes of their customers and can react quickly to change in customer buying habits.

What to look for, Market research should investigate four areas: customers, customer needs, competition, and trends. The research conducted should answer questions like:

Customers. Identify their:

* Age

* Income

* Occupation

* Family size

* Marital status

* Residence

•Interests and hobbies

Customers wants

* Is the product needed for a limited time (diapers, for example)?

* Are customers looking for quicker service?

* Do customers want guarantees with the products?

* Will customer come frequently (for example a grocery store) or seldom (a car dealership)?

* Are customers looking for a wider distribution or more convenient locations?

Competition

* What is the competitions' market share?

* How much sales volume do they do?

* How many similar firms exist?

* What attracts customers to them?

•What strengths do they advertise?

Trends. Are there:

* Population shifts? (Baby boom, for example) Legal or regulatory developments?

* Changes in the local economic situation?

* Lifestyle changes? (single parents, working women, smaller family size)

Where to get it

There are two general sources of information that can be gathered: data already available and data that can be collected by the business.

The following sources may provide already accessible data:

* Local area Chamber of Commerce

* Trade associations in the line of business

* Professional market research services

* Local library

Data can also be obtained by the business' own research efforts through the following means:

* Telephone surveys

* Local and national newspapers

* Surveys sent by mail

* Questionnaires

* Local TV and radio stations

* Interviewing

* Customer service cards

Market research doesn't have to be sophisticated and expensive. While money can be spent to collect research data, there are many inexpensive ways to collect this data that are easily accessible to the small business owner. Several of these methods are:

Employees. This is one of the best sources of information about customer likes and dislikes. Usually employees work more directly with customers and hear complaints that may not make it to the owner. They are also aware of the items customers request that the business doesn't offer. They can probably also give a pretty good customer profile from their day-to-day contacts. Customers. Talk to the customers to get a feel for you clientele, and ask them where improvements can be made. Encouraging and collecting customer comments and suggestions is an effective form of research. By asking the customers to explain how the product could improve to fill their needs, constructive market research is done, as well as instilling customer confidence in the product.

Competition. Monitoring the competition can be a valuable source of information. Their activities may provide important information about customer demand that were overlooked, and they may be capturing part of the market by offering something unique. Likewise, small business owners can capitalize on unique points of their products that the competition does not offer. Company records and files. Looking at company records and files can be very informative. Look at sales records, complaints, receipts, or any other records that can show you where your customers live or work or how and what they buy. One small business owner found that addresses on cash receipts allowed the pinpointing of customers in his market area. With this kind of information he could cross reference his customers' address and the products they purchased. From this information he was able to check the effectiveness of his advertising placement. However, realize that this information represents the past. Present or future trends may mean that past information is too obsolete to be effective.

Your customers' addresses alone can tell you a lot about them. You can pretty closely guess your customers' lifestyle by knowing what the neighborhoods they live in are like. Knowing how they live can give you solid hints on what they can be expected to buy.

In addition, check returned items to see if there is a pattern. Check company files to determine which items sell best, and which sell poorly.

The key to effective marketing research is neither technique nor data it's useful information. Customers likes and dislikes are shifting constantly so this information must be timely. It's much better to get there on time with a little than too late with a lot.

A MARKET STRATEGY

With the research information gathered, the next step is to develop a market strategy. Use this information to determine areas where the competition doesn't adequately fill consumer demand or areas where a new product or different product promotion would capture part of the market.

A new business may capture a significant market share by aiming their market strategy on areas not focused on by the competition.

Some examples of the various areas of emphasis include offering a:

* Better or wider distribution

* Specialized instead of a broad product line (or vise versa)

* Lower price

* Modified product (improved)

* Better value for the consumers money (quality)

* More dependable product or service

* Customer support service

As a new business can enter an industry and capture a share

of the market, an established business can use the same strategies to increase their market share as well.

TARGET MARKETING

When the marketing strategy is developed, determine with which customer group this would be most effective. For example, a "better value for the money" may be more appealing to the "family" consumer group while a "wider distribution" would be more attractive to consumers who travel. Remember that different market strategies may appeal to different target markets. Therefore, apply the collected data to choose the combinations that will work best. The market is defined by different segments.

Some examples are:

* Geographic: Specialize products to customers who live in certain neighborhoods or regions, or under particular climates.

* Demographic: Direct advertising to families, retired people, or to the occupation of consumers.

* Psychographic: Target promotion to the opinions or attitudes of the customers (political or religious, for example).

* Product benefits: Aim marketing to emphasize the benefits of the product or service that would appeal to consumers who buy for this reason in particular (low cost or easy access, for example).

* Previous customers: Identify and promote to those groups who have purchased the product before.

THE MARKETING MIX

Before the marketing mix decision is made, determine what purpose these marketing efforts are going to serve. Are they to:

* Deepen the customer base?

* Increase the market share? If so, by how much?

* Increase sales? If so, by how much?

* Reach new geographic markets?

* Increase customer traffic?

* Sell remaining inventory to prepare for a new product line?

After these objectives are established, determine a date for accomplishing the objective. The marketing mix allows owner-managers to combine different marketing decision areas such as products and services, promotion and advertising, pricing, and place to construct an overall marketing program.

Products and Services

Use the product or service itself as a marketing resource. Having something unique provides motivation behind advertising. While the ideas mentioned under market strategy apply here, another option is to change or modify the product or service. Additional attention may be given to a product if it has changed color, size, or style, while a service may draw similar attention by modifying the services provided. Remember sales and promotional opportunities are generated by product differentiation.

Promotion and Advertising

With a marketing strategy and clear objectives outlined, use advertising to get the message out to customers.

Advertising can be done through:

* Online (Google Adwords, Social media, etc.)

* The yellow pages

* A press release

* Sponsoring a civic event or activity

* The newspaper

* Billboards or posters

* Flyers or handbills

* Direct mail advertising

*The radio

One element of advertising is promotional activities. These activities not only advertise, but they offer added incentive for customer patronage.

Some examples are:

* 2 for 1 offers

* Coupons

* Special sale prices

* Rebates

* Sweepstakes

* Give-aways

Try to reach the largest number of people with the money allocated to advertising and promotion. This may be accomplished by using several different methods of advertising. Remember to be creative and implement ideas.

Pricing

Determining price levels and pricing policies is the major factor affecting revenue. Factors such as the demand for the good, the market price, and customer responsiveness to price changes influence the price levels. Other factors such as a convenient location or more personalized service may allow a small business to charge a higher price. Make sure your price is competitive, however, by checking to see what competitors' prices are.

Place

The manufacturer and wholesaler must decide how to distribute their products. Working through established distributors or manufacturers' agent generally is most feasible for small manufacturers. Small retailers should consider cost and traffic flow as two major factors in location site selection, especially since advertising and rent can be reciprocal. In other words, low-cost, low-customer traffic location means you must spend more on advertising to build traffic.

The nature of the product or service also is important in locational decisions. If purchases are made largely on impulse (e.g., flavored popcorn), then high customer traffic and visibility are critical. On the other hand, location is less a concern for products or services that customers are willing to go out of their way to find (e.g., restaurant suppliers). The recent availability of highly segmented mailing lists (purchased from list brokers, magazines, or other companies) has enabled small businesses to operate anywhere - and serve national or international markets.

MARKETING PERFORMANCE

After the marketing mix decision is implemented, the next step is to evaluate performance. With a detailed list of company objectives, monitor how well the decisions are developing.

Evaluate objectives such as:

* Market share. Has the increased share been captured?

* Sales Volume. Was the increase reached?

* Strategy. Did the combinations of target markets and

strategy work effectively? Which ones didn't?

Also, evaluate the following decisions and others:

* Did advertising efforts reach the target groups?

* Were promotions timely?

* Did customers respond to sales, coupons, or rebates?

Additionally, consider the following:

* Is the company doing all it can to satisfy the customer?

* Do the employees make sure the customer's needs are truly satisfied, leading to the vial repeat purchase and customer loyalty?

* Is it easy for customers to find what they want at a competitive price?

* If these objectives were not reached, what were the reasons?

* If they worked well, what elements were most effective?

By evaluating performance after decisions, there is reference for future decision-making, based on past results. In addition, periodically assess customers' feelings and opinions toward the business and how well their needs are being satisfied. This can be done through surveys, customer comment cards, or simply by asking them, "How are we doing?"

Assessing performance and asking for customer input

brings us back around market research again. Your marketing plan is a continuous effort to identify and adapt to changes in markets, customer taste, and the economy for the success of your small business.

3. Twenty Seven Tips to Increase the Effectiveness of Your Delegation

Derived from Latin, delegate means "to send from." When delegating you are sending the work "from" you "to" someone else. Effective delegation Skills will not only give you more time to work on your important opportunities, but you will also help others on your team learn new skills. Here are some tips that will help you improve your delegation skills - delegation of work .

1. Delegation helps people grow underneath you in an organization and thus pushes you even higher in management. It provides you with more time, and you will be able to take on higher priority projects.

2. Delegate whole pieces or entire job pieces rather than simply tasks and activities.

3. Clearly define what outcome is needed, then let individuals use some creative thinking of their own as to how to get to that outcome.

4. Clearly define limits of authority that go with the delegated job. Can the person hire other people to work with them? Are there spending constraints?

5. Clear standards of performance will help the person know when he or she is doing exactly what is expected.

6. When on the receiving end of delegation, work to make your boss' job easier and to get the boss promoted. This will enhance your promotability also.

7. Assess routine activities in which you are involved. Can any of them be eliminated or delegated?

8. Never underestimate a person's potential. Delegate slightly more than you think the person is capable of handling. Expect them to succeed, and you will be pleasantly surprised more frequently than not.

9. Expect completed staff work from the individuals reporting to you. That is, they will come to you giving you alternatives and suggestions when a problem exists rather than just saying "Boss, what should we do?"

10. Do not avoid delegating something because you cannot give someone the entire project. Let the person start with a bite size piece, then after learning and doing that, they can accept larger pieces and larger areas of responsibility.

11. Agree on a monitoring or measurement procedure that will keep you informed as to progress on this project because you are ultimately still responsible for it and need to know that it is progressing as it should. In other words- If you can't measure it don't delegate it.

12. Keep your mind open to new ideas and ways of doing things. There just might be a better way than the way something has previously been done.

13. Delegation is not giving an assignment. You are asking

the person to accept responsibility for a project. They have the right to say no.

14. Encourage your people to ask for parts of your job.

15. Never take back a delegated item because you can do it better or faster. Help the other person learn to do it better.

16. Agree on the frequency of feedback meetings or reports between yourself and the person to whom you are delegating. Good communication will assure ongoing success.

17. Delegation strengthens your position. It shows you are doing your job as a manager-getting results with others. This makes you more promotable.

18. Delegation is taking a risk that the other person might make a mistake, but people learn from mistakes and will be able to do it right the next time. Think back to a time a project was delegated to you and you messed it up. You also learned a valuable lesson.

19. Find out what the talents and interests of your people are and you will be able to delegate more intelligently and effectively.

20. A person will be more excited about doing a project when they came up with the idea of how to do it, than if the boss tells them how to do it.

21. Be sensitive to upward delegation by your staff. When they ask you for a decision on their project, ask them to

think about some alternatives which you will then discuss with them. This way responsibility for action stays with the staff member.

22. Don't do an activity that someone else would be willing to do for you if you would just ask them.

23. "Push" responsibility down in a caring helpful way.

24. Remember, you are not the only one that can accomplish an end result. Trust others to be capable of achieving it.

25. Break large jobs into manageable pieces and delegate pieces to those who can do them more readily.

26. Keep following up and following through until the entire project is done.

27. Resist the urge to solve someone else's problem. They need to learn for themselves. Give them suggestions and perhaps limits but let them take their own action.

4. How to Reach Your Goals Faster

Life is a journey. Not just any journey, but the most fantastic journey in the universe. Life is a journey from where you are to where you want to be. You can choose your own destination. Not only that, you can choose how you are going to get there. Goal setting will help you end up where you want to be.

-- When it comes to setting goals, start off with what's important to you in life. Take out a sheet of paper. Sit quietly, and on that sheet of paper, brainstorm what you want to accomplish between now and the end of your life.

-- Second step-use another sheet of paper, and this time consider yourself and your personal goals for the next 12 month period. Some key areas in which you might set personal goals include: family, personal growth, financial, health, social, career, hobbies, spiritual, and recreation. Write down the things that you plan to accomplish or achieve or attain during this one-year period?

-- Now, as a third step, go back and compare the two goal lists you have made. Make sure that the items on your short-term list will, as you attain them, be helping you attain your long-term or lifetime goals. It is important that what you are doing short term is taking you in the right direction toward your lifetime goals. Please rewrite your short term goals now if you need to.

-- As a next step, looking at the goals that are on your list at this time, if there are any that you are not willing to pay the price for, go ahead and cross them out, leaving only those items you are willing to cause to happen in your life. This does not necessarily mean you have the money or the other resources for attaining the goal right now. However, when you do have it, would you spend it on or trade it for the goals you have on your list?

-- Now, on still another sheet of paper, create the job goals that are important to you during this upcoming 12-month period. Identify what outcomes you wish to attain or achieve during this one-year period in your specific area of responsibility and authority.

-- Some key areas in which you might consider writing job goals, if you did not already, include: quality, quantity, cost control, cost improvement, equipment, procedures, training, sales, financial, and personnel.

-- As a next step, look for the blending between your job or work goals and your personal goals. Anywhere you notice that you are attaining a goal on the job while at the same time you are attaining a personal goal, note this relationship: it is in these areas you will be most highly motivated.

-- For each of the three lists that you have just created, take an additional sheet of paper and list the activities that you must do to attain the most important goal that you have on each of your lists.

-- Now on another piece of paper titled "Things To-Do List" identify from the activities you just listed, the ones that you must do tomorrow to move you toward your most important goal.

-- Rewrite your goals in these categories at least every three months.

-- The only thing in life that is constant is the fact that everything is changing. It makes sense that our goals will change as we change.

-- Recognize how focusing on what you do want, what you do intend to accomplish, also defines what you choose not to do in your life.

Daily rewrite your list of "Things To-Do" after first reviewing your desired goals.

-- Success is defined as "the progressive realization of a worthwhile goal." If you are doing the things that are moving you toward the attainment of your goal, then you are "successful" even if you are not there yet.

-- Every step along the way to achieving a goal is just as important as the last step.

-- It is not the achieving of a goal that is so important, it is what you become in the process.

-- Set goals with your family also. Help children learn this process early in life.

-- Decide what you should be accomplishing and then stick to your knitting. Do not attempt to be or do all things for all people.

-- Dreams and wishes are not goals until they are written as specific end results on paper.

-- Written specific goals provide direction and focus to your activities. They become a road map to follow.

-- Being busy with activities does not pay, only results do. As in baseball you only get points for getting to the goal of home plate. Just making it to the bases does not count.

-- It has been said that the amount of information available to us is now doubling in less than 30 months. We must learn to focus on only what is truly important to our self and our job.

-- Be sure the goals and activities that you are working for are yours and that you really want and desire to achieve them. The commitment is vital to your success in achieving them.

-- When you have a goal that is exciting to you, the life energy flows through you. You are excited about accomplishing it because it is personally meaningful.

-- Create a time line or matrix chart on which you display your goals visually and the dates when you will have them accomplished.

-- Continually look for ways to integrate or blend personal and professional goals.

-- Setting a goal, that you believe is unattainable will result in frustration. To be challenging and motivating, goals must be perceived as realistic and attainable.

-- Those people with dreams are the ones most likely to experience them.

-- Set goals carefully for you will attain them. This also means if you set none, you will attain that.

-- Goals, when thoughtfully set, can provide strong motivational direction.

-- Clear cut, understandable and realistic objectives leading to the goal help to maintain the sense of realism and the hope of attainment of the goal.

-- Establish measurement criteria to monitor progressive movement toward your goal. Then you will experience progress.

-- Set goals that you will be proud to have achieved, then sense your having completed them.

-- Have a vision that you know is unquestionably right and you will be internally driven to achieve that vision.

-- A goal is "reasonable" when you can see the entire process needed to get to its attainment.

-- Good planning assists in sensing reasonableness of

challenging goals.

-- Use picture goals.

-- Develop an emotional reason why you should attain your goal.

5. How to Deal with Changes in The Market

The winds of change are building...reshaping business, government, educational institutions, not for profit groups, civic and professional groups, the military and all of our personal lives. Some people dig in their heels and try to resist change. Others ride the winds of change and seize the amazing opportunities it brings. Use these ten habits to recognize and maximize the gifts of change.

1. Accept the Certainty of Uncertainty.

Change scares a lot of people. Facing the unknown rattles our nerves and undermines confidence. Yet, our rapidly world if filled with ambiguity, shifting priorities, different expectations, unanswered questions, and new responsibilities. People with a high need for closure and structure find it especially difficult. The ability to cope with uncertainty and ambiguity are critical skills for success in our New World.

2. Become A Quick Change Artist.

Hundreds of thousands of years ago, this planet was inhabited by powerful dinosaurs. Then, something happened and in a very short time the great beasts perished. While scientists don't agree about what exactly happened, they do agree that whatever it was the dinosaurs simply could not adapt to the change. There are plenty of human dinosaurs out there today saying..."Don't rock the boat"....."why change what's working?....and "That's not the way we've always done it." Resistance to change is a dead-end street. Change requires that we abandon the status quo, overcome our additions to comfort zones, and adapt quickly to new situations and ways of doing things.

3. Stay In School.

The most effective way to cope with change and find the opportunities it offers is to NEVER STOP LEARNING. We are the sum of what we read, hear and experience...the thousands of bits of information we pick up from many sources. Successful lifelong learners make it a point to learn something New everyday, to gain ideas from everyplace they go and everyone they meet. A great way to do this is to commit to the 30/10 RULE. Commit 30 minutes per day to actively seeking new information and then take an additional 10 minutes to decide how to apply this new information to your life. COACHU resources make the 30/10 Rule easy!

4. Open Your Mind and Unhook Your Personal Prejudices.

A prejudice is a judgment or opinion reached before the facts are known or maintained long after the facts have changed. Prejudices severely limit our ability to respond to change. Prejudices stifle our creativity and innovation. Seek out diversity. Read books and magazines about subjects you have never been interested in before. Seek out new friends and acquaintances of different cultures, ages, and thinking styles and learn from them.

5. Become A Trend Watcher and New Idea Collector.

Opportunities abound in trends and change. Look at magazines, newspapers, the Net, and other sources for themes that show up on a regular basis. Pay special attention to feature sections in publications like USA Today and Entrepreneur Magazine. Start an Idea File.

6. Be Sure To Open All Your Gifts and Look For More.

It is so much fun to open gifts...especially ones we didn't know we were getting. We all have many gifts we have never fully used. Talents, abilities, and potential we have never exercised and developed. High achievers in a changing world use all their gifts and constantly seek new ones. For every gift you open, there are many more waiting to be discovered and used.

7. Cultivate and Maintain a Strong Resource Network.

Your Team 100, Circle of Ten or a Personal Advisory Board are all part of your resource network. Become a Master Networker. Your network is a gold mine of resources and support. Remember networking is a reciprocal process. It is about getting and giving.

8. Develop a Reputation as FIXER...not a Finger Pointer.

Every business, every organization, every community and even our own families need people who are willing to take care of problems, not merely point them out. People who are objective and willing to explore many options and solutions, rather than automatically opposing anything that even smells like change, become very valuable. Make it a rule never to complain without offering solutions along with your problem.

9. Lighten Up! Optimism is Contagious.

The benefits of optimism and a sense of humor cannot be overestimated in a climate of change and chaos. Negativity and its by-product, stress, cloud judgment and interfere with objectivity. On the other hand, a well-developed sense of humor increases optimism and helps us prevent blowing things out of proportion. We must consider how many other people take their cues from us. Do you lead others optimistically into change or do you somehow lead them into resistance? Optimism is contagious...spread it every chance you get.

10. Stop Waiting!

Many people can make an entire lifetime out of getting ready to do something...laying the groundwork...making plans...waiting until the time is "right." Change doesn't wait and in today's competitive world, waiting is a luxury we can no longer afford. We need to develop a sense of urgency ...coupled with action. The best insurance policy for tomorrow is the best use of today. CARPE DIEM!

6. How to Build a Winning Team

You've just been in a serious car accident. You've got massive internal injuries and a broken jaw. You're going to be in the hospital at least a month. Your jaw is wired shut so you can't use the phone. Will your business run easily and well while you recover? Will your customers be served while you are gone? If you've just experienced heart failure over this prospect, the following list is for you. The information below, if put into practice, will reduce your stress, increase your business' productivity, and give you the vacation you so richly deserve. Here's the top ten things you can do to make your business run as smoothly as possible.

1. Hire wisely

Most businesses hire bodies for particular jobs rather than people to help build a future. Your business is only as good as each individual employee's contribution to its functioning. Therefore, look for the three i's when you hire: intelligence, initiative, and integrity. For every position, from receptionist to packing clerk, hire only the best you can find. Conversely, if you have current employees who are not performing well, consider whether they are a wise investment of your money.

2. Build a team, not your ego

Many employers let their egos dominate their interactions

with their employees. Stop the pattern. Instead, trust your employees to do their jobs. Make each employee feel that they are an invaluable member of the company team. Let each employee know they are an integral part of the company's end product. Set the example for positive interaction at all times between members of the team even when ideas or performance must be corrected.

3. Reward well

When you get good employees, reward them financially and emotionally. Be sure their pay is at least at market rate. Take time often to acknowledge each employee's contribution. The two biggest loyalty builders are two simple words-- thank you.

4. Be hands on

Know each employee's job and how to do it. This not only gives you an automatic reserve employee and trainer (yourself), but has an added bonus. If you show an employee that you are willing to learn or have learned his/her job, you are communicating that you believe their work has value. Every employee needs to know that whether they are emptying trash cans, setting the presses, or selling the large accounts, their work is worthwhile and valuable.

5. Make your employees versatile

In a small company, every employee should know how to do at least two jobs, particularly on the technical and service sides. For critical tasks, at least three employees should know how to do each job. Thus, you always have an on-the-premises reserve who can step in when needed.

6. Give away tasks, but not ultimate leadership

What is it you do best? Are you the idea man, the best salesman in your company, the organizer? Find your best talent and then delegate all other tasks to your employees. Train them appropriately to do their job, let them know you have confidence in their ability to perform well, and then let them do their jobs. Adding responsibility with confidence will increase your employee's willingness to work and their pride in the company's end result. At the same time, you must maintain ultimate leadership. In any well run ship, the captain makes final decisions and you are still the captain, albeit a benign one.

7. Communicate, communicate, communicate

You must talk with your employees, solicit their suggestions, and positively correct their mistakes. Conversely, you must create an atmosphere where employees are willing and able to talk with you. The two best sources of information on how your business is doing and how to improve it are your employees and your customers. Pay attention to both.

8. Give your best and always and encourage the same in your employees

Pride in the company and its product or service always begins at the top. If you give a half effort or let a sloppily produced product go out the door to a client, you are sending a message to your employees that you do not respect your clients or your work. Your employees will adopt that view as well. If you set the example of giving the extra effort, pitching in when needed, caring about your fellow team members, working as a unit to be the best in your particular business, and taking care of the bottom line, your employees worth having and keeping will follow suit.

9. Encourage innovation and creation

Give your employees a stake in the future. Once a month, have a meeting where the employees make suggestions on how to improve your product, service, efficiency, or bottom line. Give monetary rewards when the ideas produce increases to the bottom line. Give positive encouragement for the process.

10. Have a second in command

No general goes into battle without a major who can take over if he is felled by a bullet. You are your business' general and must act accordingly. Find someone you trust within your company who has the same goals, ideals, and a similar business style. Train him/her appropriately. Let others know he/she has your confidence and authority when you are gone. When that is done, leave on vacation and test the theory out. If you have completed steps 1-9 above, your business will run easily and well and you will have regained a healthy balance in your life.

7. How to Make a Good First Impression

We sometimes get only one chance to make an impression on someone either in our personal or business life. Therefore it is important to remember some basic things to do that will assure us of making the best impression possible. The following are ten of the most common things people can do to make the best first impression possible.

1. Appear Neat And Dress Appropriately.

Being neat in our appearance is something we can do regardless of whether we are trying to make a good impression on someone or not. In a *first meeting* situation for business, to show up in jeans, tennis shoes and with uncombed hair would be a big mistake. If the situation is social, dressing casual is fine depending on where you are meeting, but being well groomed is always going to make a good impression.

2. Maintain Good Eye Contact.

From the first time you meet the person unlit you part, maintain good direct eye contact with them. This usually indicates to people that you are listening to them, interested in them, and friendly. You need not stare or glare at them. Simply focus on them and their immediate direction the majority of the time. When talking, look at them also, since your new acquaintance wants to be sure you are talking to him/her and not the floor. It also will give you an idea of how the person is receiving what you are saying to them if you are looking at them.

3. Shake Their Hand At The Beginning And When Parting.

Whether it is a business meeting or a social occasion, most people appreciate or expect a friendly handshake. The best kind are firm (no need to prove your strength) and 3-5 seconds long. Pumping up and down or jerking their arm about is not needed nor usually welcomed. A *limp rag* handshake is not recommended unless you have good reason to believe shaking the person's hand any harder would injure them. Look at them in the eye when shaking their hand.

4. SMILE! :-)

A smile goes a long way in making a first impression. When you shake hands with the person, smile as you introduce yourself or say hello. Even if the other person does not smile, you can, and it will be remembered by the other person. As you talk or listen to the person speak, smile off and on to show your interest, amusement, or just to show you are being friendly.

5. Listen More Than You Talk.

Unless you are asked for your life story (in which case give a very abbreviated version) let the other person do most of the talking as you listen. Listening to your new acquaintance will give you information to refer to later, and it will give your new friend the impression you are genuinely interested in them, their business, etc. If you are asked questions, feel free to talk. If you are really bored, avoid 3-5 word sentence replies to your companion's questions. Pretend at least to be interested. You won't/don't necessarily ever have to talk with this person again.

6. Relax And Be Yourself.

Who else would you be? Well, sometimes people try to act differently than they normally would to impress or show off to a new acquaintance. Putting on facades and *airs* is not recommended, as a discerning person will sense it and it will have a negative affect on how they view you. Just be yourself and relax and *go with the flow* of conversation.

7. Ask Them About *Their* Business And Personal Life.

Show that you have an active interest in the other person's professional and personal life. When an appropriate time comes, ask them to tell you about their family and their business if they have not already done so. People love to talk about themselves. They usually feel flattered and respected when others, especially people who have never met them, show real interest in their business and their personal life. It also shows that you are not self-centered when you do not spend alot of time talking about yourself and *your* life.

8. Don't *Name Drop* Or Brag.

Very few people you will meet for the first time will be favorably impressed if you start telling them you know Donald Trump, Don Johnson, or the CEO of Widgits, Inc. They want to get to know you and have you get to know them. Experienced and secure business people are not impressed by who you know as much as what you know. If someone asks you if you know *so and so*, then it's appropriate to tell them the truth. Unless they do, it sounds like you are very insecure and trying to really *impress them*. Bragging about your financial, business or social coups or feats is likewise in bad taste and not recommended. Just keep it simple and factual and be yourself.

9. Don't Eat Or *Drink* Too Much.

If your first meeting is at a function or place where food and alcohol are served, it is wise to eat and drink in moderation. This is especial true of drinking alcohol! You want to be able to listen well and remember what is said, and speak well for yourself. There is probably nothing that leaves a worse first impression on a business or social date than for their new *acquaintance* to get intoxicated and to say or do things that are embarrassing, rude, crude, or all three. Use good self control and eat as your new friend does, and drink only in social moderation or not at all. What is done one night under the influence of alcoholic merriment might be regretted for hundreds of nights in clear headed sobriety!

10. Part With A Smile, A Handshake And A Sincere Comment Or Compliment.

Regardless of how you felt the evening went it is simply common courtesy to shake hands when the evening is over, offer a smile and some sort of friendly comment or compliment. If it was a social evening and you had a great time, offer a sincere compliment and let them know you'd like to meet again. If it was a business meeting, offer a smile and a sincere comment around how it was nice to meet them, get to know them, learn about their business etc. You may never have to see the person again, but they may know people who they will tell about their meeting with you who you *will* work with or need to meet down the road. It always pays to be kind and polite even if you were not treated that way or did not enjoy the time you spent with someone.

8. How to Manage Your Business Successfully

Manage a business successfully, manage a company, is the key to the establishment and growth of the business. The key to successful management is to examine the marketplace environment and create employment and profit opportunities that provide the potential growth and financial viability of the business.

Despite the importance of management, this area is often misunderstood and poorly implemented, primarily because people focus on the output rather than the process of management.

Toward the end of the 1980s, business managers became absorbed in improving product quality, sometimes ignoring their role vis-a-vis personnel. The focus was on reducing costs and increasing output, while ignoring the long-term benefits of motivating personnel. This shortsighted view tended to increase profits in the short term, but created a dysfunctional long-term business environment.

Simultaneously with the increase in concern about quality, entrepreneurship attracted the attention of business. A sudden wave of successful entrepreneurs seemed to render earlier management concepts obsolete. The popular press focused on the new cult heroes Steve Jobs and Steve Wozniack (creators and developers of the Apple Computer) while ignoring the marketing and organizing talents of Mike Markula, the executive responsible for

Apple's business plan. The story of two guys selling their Volkswagen bus to build the first Apple computer was more romantic than that of the organizational genius that enabled Apple to develop, market and ship its products while rapidly becoming a major corporation.

In large businesses, effective manage business skills requires planning. Planning is essential for developing a firm's potential. However, many small businesses do not recognize the need for long-range plans, because the small number of people involved in operating the business implies equal responsibility in the planning and decision-making processes. Nevertheless, the need for planning is as important in a small business as it is in a large one.

This guide focuses on the importance of good management practices. Specifically, it addresses the responsibilities of managing the external and internal environments.

Managing A Business Effectively: The External Environment

Five decades ago, Alvin Toffler suggested that the vision of the citizen in the tight grip of an omnipotent bureaucracy would be replaced by an organizational structure of ad-hocracy. The traditional business organization implied a social contract between employees and employers. By adhering to a fixed set of obligations and sharply defined roles and responsibilities, employees received a predefined set of rewards.

The organizational structure that Toffler predicted in 1970 became the norm 20 years later, and with it came changed concepts of authority. As organizations became more transitory, the authority of the organization and firm was replaced by the authority of the individual manager. This entrepreneurial management model is now being replicated throughout society. As a result, the individual business owner must internalize ever increasing organizational functions.

Another change in today's business environment is dealing with government agencies. Their effect on the conduct of business most recently appears to have increased. As industries fail to achieve high levels of ethical behavior or individual businesses exhibit specific lapses, the government rushes in to fill the breach with its regulations.

Managing A Small Business Effectively: The Internal Environment

HUMAN RESOURCE ISSUES

Ensuring Open Communications

Effective communications play an integral role in managing and operating any successful business. With open communications changes and their effects on the organization are quickly shared. Your firm then has the time and skills needed to respond to changes and take advantage of evolving opportunities.

The following checklist addressing how you would respond to an employee's suggestion provides an assessment of the communication process in your business. Place a check next to the statements that are commonly heard in your business.

Statement

Face facts it's unrealistic. -----

Who else has done it? -----

It's not your problem. -----

Fill out form XX/xx revised. -----

It won't work. -----

Bring it to the committee. -----

We don't have the time. -----

We tried it before and it failed. -----

You think what? You're joking! -----

Everybody knows that that's foolish. -----

We can't afford to think about it. -----

Don't you have better things to do? -----

Are you some kind of a radical? -----

We're too small/big for that. -----

Impossible; our main product line would be obsolete. -----

The boss would never consider it. -----

It's contrary to company policy. -----

Carefully consider any statements that you have checked. This may indicate that management is inflexible and unresponsive to employee suggestions. Management that is unable to respond immediately to changes in the market signals an inflexible unstable firm. In the rapidly changing business environment such management can mean eventual failure for your business. If you haven't developed such a checklist do so. It will help you determine if and where adjustments are needed in your management staff.

Balancing Schedules Stress and Personnel

Without organization and good management the compressed time schedules associated with modern business can cause stress and make extraordinary demands on people. An effective management structure can reduce stress and channel the productive capacity of employees into business growth and profits.

Setting Duties Tasks and Responsibilities

An organization is characterized by the nature and determination of employees' duties tasks and responsibilities. While many organizations use different methods for determining these it is essential that they be clearly defined.

The core of any organization is its people and their functions. Duties tasks and responsibilities often evolve in an ad hoc manner. A typical firm starts with a few people often one performing all duties. As the firm grows others are hired to fill specific roles often on a functional basis. Roles that were handled by consultants and specialists outside the firm now are handled internally. As new needs emerge new roles are developed.

Just as an emerging business develops an accounting system it should also develop a human resource system. For instance the following employee information should be available and checked for accuracy at least once each year.

- Name

- Address

- Nationality (immigration status)

- Marital status and dependents

- Hire date

- Company job history:

- Title and code

- Performance

- Location

- Salary rate and history

- Education including degrees

- Specialty training

- Transcripts as appropriate

- Pre-employment work experience:

- Key responsibilities and levels

- Professional licenses or certificates

- Professional publication and speaking engagements

- Teaching experience

- Language abilities:

- Reading

- Writing

- Speaking

- Leadership evidence:

- Company

- Civic

- Other

- Relocation preferences and limitations

- Travel experience and preferences

- Career goals

Review your personnel files periodically to ensure that the information is correct and current. Implement a system that will make updating personnel files a fairly simple routine yet confidential process.

Managing a Business Effectively: Building Your Team

The apex of an effective organization lies in developing the business team. Such a team involves delegating authority and increasing productivity. Assess the effectiveness of your business team with the following checklist:

The leader of the team is respected by the members. -----

The abilities of all team members are respected. -----

A team spirit is evident through activities. -----

Individual members compensate for weaknesses in each other. -----

Jokes are not disparaging. -----

A genuine feeling of being part of the best is exuded. -----

The work area is self-delineated and reflects a spirit. -----

Mistakes result in corrective action not retribution. -----

Each member understands the importance of his or her contribution. -----

The team can explore new areas of activity. -----

Security of employment is evident. -----

Controlling Conflict

Another key to successful management lies in controlling conflict. Conflict cannot be eliminated from either the business or the interpersonal activities of the enterprise. A measure of the organization's success is the degree to which conflict can be exposed and the energies associated with it channeled to develop the firm. Although establishing policies and procedures represents the tangible aspect of organization and management the mechanisms to tolerate and embody challenges to the established operation serve as the real essence of a firm that will survive and prosper.

How to Manage a Business Successfully: Structural Issues

Organization

The effectiveness of a particular organizational form depends on a variety of internal and external events for example:

- Competitors (number or activity)
- Technology (internal or external)
- Regulatory environment
- Customer characteristics
- Supplier characteristics
- Economic environment
- Key employees
- Growth
- Strategy (including new products and markets)

Even though you may discover that certain events are affecting your business be careful not to change the organizational structure of your firm without discussing it with your management team. Employees generally can accomplish goals despite organizational structures imposed by management. Because restructuring involves spending a lot of time learning new rules implementing a new organizational structure is costly.

Structure

The essence of a successful organization can be more simply summarized than implemented. The following checklist can help you determine measures to ensure your management structure is adequate. Check the entries that apply to your firm and also find out what measures your company needs to take to improve its management structure.

- Key market and customers are understood. -----
- Technology is mastered. -----
- Key objectives are articulated and shared. -----
- Major functions are identified and staffed. -----
- A hierarchy of relationships is established. -----
- A business team is in place and functioning. -----
- Measurable results are well above industry standards. -----
- Employees are the best source of new hires. -----

Policy and Procedural Issues in Managing a Business

Authority

The central element of organizational management is authority. Through authority your firm develops the structure necessary to achieve its objectives.

A. L. Stinchcombe summarized the role of authority succinctly when he stated any administrative system that decides on the use of resources is also a system of authority directing the activities of people.

The authority that once was conferred by either owning a small business or having a position in the bureaucracy of a larger firm has been replaced by technical competence (including that of forming and running the business). Forces external to your business may emphasize the elements of granted versus earned authority. Once the owner-manager controlled the entire business but suppliers customers unions and the government have severely limited the ability of the business owner-manager to take independent action.

A primary component of authority is the exercise of control within the organization. A thorough system of controls ensures the firm's operation and provides a mechanism for imposing authority. Internal controls include the provision that authority be delegated and circumscribed; examples of these provisions follow. Place a check by the provisions that apply to your firm. Consider implementing controls over areas that you have not checked.

- Approval for disbursements of cash and regular accounting. -----
- Reconciliation of bank statements. -----
- Periodic count and reconciliation of inventory records. -----
- Approval of pricing policies and exemptions. -----
- Approval of credit policies and exemptions. -----
- Review of expense and commission accounts. -----
- Approval of purchasing and receiving policies. -----
- Review of payments to vendors and employees. -----

- Approval of signature authorities for payments. -----
- Review of policies. -----

Delegation is a key to the effective exercise of authority in your business. By delegating limited authority to accomplish specific tasks the talents of employees in the organization can be used to upgrade the skills and experience of the manager. The following checklist enables you to determine if you are taking advantage of opportunities to delegate authority.

Is your time consumed by daily chores? -----

Do you have time for the following:

- Training and development of subordinates? -----

- Planning? -----

- Coordinating and controlling work of subordinates? -----

- Visiting customers and subordinates regularly? -----

- Remaining involved in new product development? -----

- Visiting branch locations regularly? -----

- Attending business meetings outside your business? -----

- Participating in civic affairs? -----

Is no one on your staff as good as you are? -----

To effectively delegate responsibility and authority in your organization you must:

- Accept the power of delegation.
- Know the capabilities of subordinates.
- Ensure that specific training is available.
- Select specific responsibilities to be delegated.
- Clearly define the extent and limits of delegation.
- Match each with necessary authority.
- Provide periodic monitoring and interest.
- Restrain the impulse to insist on how to do something.
- Remember there are many ways to accomplish a specific objective.
- Assess results and provide appropriate feedback.
- Praise and criticize.

The skills and abilities of each level of authority can be increased by effectively delegating authority throughout any organization.

Operating Reports

Operating reports form the organizational basis of your business. Such reports mirror the organization its structure and function. They define key relationships between employees and can either minimize or increase organizational stress.

For many businesses the following reports form the basis for analyzing the specific areas of a business (the frequency of each report depends on the nature size and organization of your business). Check the reports your firm currently generates.

Consider creating reporting systems where they are lacking.

- Case reports (daily, weekly, monthly) -----

- New orders and backlog (weekly, monthly) -----
- Shipments/sales (weekly, monthly) -----
- Employment (monthly) -----
- Inventory out of stock (weekly, monthly) -----
- Product quality (weekly, monthly) -----
- Accounts receivable aging accounts (monthly) -----
- Weekly overdue accounts -----
- Returns and allowances (monthly) -----
- Production (weekly, monthly) -----

Reporting must be kept current to allow for timely identification and correction of problems before serious damage to the organization occurs.

Too much reporting as well as inappropriate reporting can be as destructive as too little reporting. For instance the CEO of a major industrial firm who receives daily production and inventory reports by model can lose his or her ability to maintain an overall perspective. Thus operating managers must attempt to identify and solve local problems and take advantage of local opportunities within their own authority. Inappropriate reporting compromises management's ability to leverage individual skills and abilities.

Operating reports not only provide essential data that enable management to accomplish its objectives they also focus staff's attention on the organization's goals. If reporting is not taken seriously employees may deal with customers suppliers and each other in a similarly trivial manner.

To avoid inappropriate reporting review reporting policies annually to ensure that reports are appropriate and contain the information needed to make sound management decisions.

Conclusion

Successful management is founded on the mastery of a myriad of details. While management schools teach the importance of focusing attention on major issues affecting the business practical managers realize the major issues are the variety of small aspects that form the business. In an increasingly structured society inattention to even one minor detail can result in significant disruption of the business or even its failure.

How To Manage A Small Business: Checklist For An Effective Organization

The following checklist will help you identify and determine the effectiveness of the management and organizational structure of the firm. If you answer yes to most of the following questions you are effectively managing your firm. A no answer indicates that you need to focus on this management issue.

yes/no

- Are responsibilities clear and matched by authority? -----
- Is your business structure clear yet flexible? -----
- Are communications focused on finding solutions rather than placing blame? -----
- Do people have the information and resources necessary to do an excellent job? -----
- Do you and your employees care about the business? -----

- Does staff come in early and stay late on their own initiative? -----
- Are mechanisms for conflict resolution working? -----
- Is disorder minimized and channeled? -----
- Can people joke with and about each other and you? -----
- Does a corporate plan spell out the firm's vision? -----
- Do employees pitch in unasked during a crisis? -----
- Do customers and suppliers prefer to do business with you? -----

9. Financial Management Essentials

Making a profit is the most important - some might say the only - objective of a business. Profit measures success. It can be defined simply: Revenues - Expenses = Profit. So, to increase profits you must raise revenues, lower expenses, or both. To make improvements you must know what's really going on financially at all times. You have to watch every financial event without any kind of optimistic filter.

This financial management analysis Guide is a series of questions with comments to help you analyze your profits, their sufficiency and trend, the contribution of each of your product lines or services to them, and to help you determine if you have the kind of record system you need. The questions and comments are not meant to be definitive presentations on the subjects. They are meant to point to areas where further study might be - well - profitable.

Are You making A Profit?

Financial Analysis of Revenues and Expenses

Since profit is revenues less expenses, to determine what your profit is you must first identify all revenues and expenses for the period under study.

1. Have you chosen an appropriate period for profit determination?

For accounting purposes firms generally use a twelve month period, such as January 1 to December 31 or July 1 to June 30. The accounting year you select doesn't have to be a calendar year (January to December); a seasonal business, for example, might close its year after the end of the season. The selection depends upon the nature of your business, your personal preference, or possible tax considerations.

2. Have you determined your total revenues for the accounting period?

In order to answer this question, consider the following questions:

- What is the amount of gross revenue from sales of your goods or service? (Gross Sales)
- What is the amount of goods returned by your customers and credited? (Returns and Rejects)
- What is the amount of discounts given to your customers and employees? (Discounts)
- What is the amount of net sales from goods and services? **(Net Sales =** Gross Sales - Returns and Rejects + Discounts))
- What is the amount of income from other sources, such as interest on bank deposits, dividends from securities, rent on property leased to others? (Non-operating Income)

- What is the amount of total revenue?(Total Revenue = Net Sales + Non-operating Income)

3. Do you know what your total expenses are?

Expenses are the cost of goods sold and services used in the process of selling goods or services. Some common expenses for all businesses are:

- Cost of goods sold (Cost of Goods Sold = Beginning Inventory + Purchases - Ending Inventory)
- Wages and salaries (Don't forget to include your own- at the actual rate - you'd have to pay someone else to do your job.)
- Rent
- Utilities (electricity, gas telephone, water, etc.)
- Delivery expenses
- Insurance
- Advertising and promotional costs
- Maintenance and upkeep
- Depreciation (Here you need to make sure your depreciation policies are realistic and that all depreciable items are included)
- Taxes and licenses
- Interest
- Bad debts
- Professional assistance (accountant, attorney, etc.)

There are of course, many other types of expenses, but the point is that every expense must be recorded and deducted from your revenues before you know what your profit is. Understanding your expenses is the first step toward controlling them andincreasing your profit.

Financial Ratios

A financial ratio is an expression on the relationship between two items selected from the income statement or the balance sheet. Ratio analysis helps you evaluate the weak and strong points in your financial and managerial performance.

4. Do you know your current ratio?

The current ratio (current assets divided by current debts) is a measure of the cash or near cash position (liquidity) of the firm. It tells you if you have enough cash to pay your firm's current creditors. The higher the ratio, the more liquid the firm's position is and, hence, the higher the credibility of the firm. Cash, receivables, marketable securities, and inventory are current assets. Naturally you need to be realistic in valuing receivable and inventory for a true picture of your liquidity, since some debts may be uncollectable and some stock obsolete. Current liabilities are those which must be paid in one year.

5. Do you know your quick ratio?

Quick assets are current assets minus inventory. The quick ratio (or acid-test ratio) is found by dividing quick assets by current liabilities. The purpose, again, is to test the firm's ability to meet its current obligations. This test doesn't include inventory to make it a stiffer test of the company's liquidity. It tells you if the business could meet its current obligations with quickly convertible assets should sales revenue suddenly cease.

6. Do you know your total debt to net worth ratio?

This ratio (the result of total debt divided by net worth then multiplied by 100) is a measure of how company can meet its total obligation from equity. The lower the ratio, the higher the proportion of equity relative to debt and the better the firm's credit rating will be.

7. Do you know your average collection period?

You find this ratio by dividing accounts receivable by daily credit sales. (Daily credit sales = annual credit sales divided by 360.) This ratio tells you the length of time it takes the firm to get its cash after making a sale on credit. The shorter this period the quicker the cash flow is. A longer than normal period may mean overdue and un-collectible bills. If you extend credit for a specific period (say, 30 days), this ratio should be very close to the same number of day. If it's much longer than the established period, you may need to alter your credit policies. It's wise to develop an aging schedule to gauge the trend of collections (without adequate financing charges) hurt your profit, since you could be doing something much more useful with your money, such as taking advantage of discounts on your own payables.

8. Do you know your ratio of net sales to total assets?

This ratio (net sales divided by total assets) measures the

efficiency with which you are using your assets. A higher than normal ratio indicates that the firm is able to generate sales from its assets faster (and better) than the average concern.

9. Do you know your operating profit to net sales ratio?

This ratio (the result of dividing operating profit by net sales and multiplying by 100) is most often used to determine the profit position relative to sales. A higher than normal ratio indicates that your sales are good, that your expenses are low, or both. Interest income and interest expense should not be included in calculating this ratio.

10. Do you know your net profit to total assets ratio?

This ratio (found by multiplying by 100 the result of dividing net profit by total assets) is often called return on investment or ROI. It focuses on the profitability of the overall operation of the firm. Thus, it allows management to measure the effects of its policies on the firm's profitability. The ROI is the single most important measure of a firm's financial position. You might say it's the bottom line for the bottom line.

11. Do you know your net profit to net worth ratio?

This ratio is found by dividing net profit by net worth and multiplying the result by 100. It provides information on the productivity of the resources the owners have committed to the firm's operations.

All ratios measuring profitability can be computed either before or after taxes, depending on the purpose of the computations. Ratios have limitations. Since the information used to derive ratios is itself based on accounting rules and personal judgments, as well as facts, the ratios cannot be considered absolute indicators of a firm's financial position. Ratios are only one means of assessing the performance of the firm and must be considered in perspective with many other measures. They should be used as a point of departure for further analysis and not as an end in themselves.

Sufficiency Of Profit

The following questions are designed to help you measure the adequacy of the profit your firm is making. Making a profit is only the first step; making enough profit to survive and growis really what business is all about.

12. Have you compared your profit with your profit goals?

13. Is it possible your goals are too high or too low?

14. Have you compared your present profits (absolute and ratios) with the profits made in the last one to three years?

15. Have you compared your profits (absolute and ratios) with profits made by similar firms in your line?2

A number of organizations publish financial ratios for various businesses, among them Dun & Bradstreet. Robert

Morris Associates, the Accounting Corporation of America, NCR Corporation, and the Bank of America. Your own trade association may also publish such studies. Remember, these published ratios are only averages. You probably want to be better than average.

Trend Of Profit

16. Have you analyzed the direction your profits have been taking?

The preceding analysis, with all their merits, report on a firm only at a single time in the past. It is not possible to use these isolated moments to indicate the trend of your firm's performance. To do a trend analysis performance indicators (absolute amounts or ratios) should be computed for several time periods (yearly for several years, for example) and the results laid out in columns side by side for easy comparison. You can then evaluate your performance, see the direction it's taking, and make initial forecasts of where it will go.

17. Does your firm sell more than one major product line or provide several distinct services?

If it does, a separate profit and ratio analysis of each should be made:

- To show the relative contribution by each product line or service;

- To show the relative burden of expenses by each product or service;
- To show which items are most profitable, which are less so, and which are losing money; and
- To show which are slow and fast moving.

Mix Of Profit

The profit analysis of each major item help you find out the strong and weak areas of your operations. They can help you to make profit-increasing decisions to drop a product line or service or to place particular emphasis behind one or another.

Records

Good records are essential. Without them a firm doesn't know where it's been, where it is, or where it's heading. Keeping records that are accurate, up-to-date, and easy to use is one of the most important functions of the owner-manager, his or her staff, and his or her outside counselors (lawyer, accountant, banker).

Basic Records

18. Do you have a general journal and/or special journals, such as one for cash receipts and disbursements?

A general journal is the basic record of the firm. Every monetary event in the life of the firm is entered in the general journal or in one of the special journals.

19. Do you prepare a sales report or analysis?

(a) Do you have sales goals by product, department, and accounting period (month, quarter, year)?

(b) Are your goals reasonable?

(c) Are you meeting your goals?

If you aren't meeting your goals, try to list the likely reasons on a sheet of paper. Such a study might include areas such as general business climate, competition, pricing, advertising, sales promotion, credit policies, and the like. Once you've identified the apparent causes you can take steps to increase sales (and profits).

Buying and Inventory System

20. Do you have a buying and inventory system?

The buying and inventory systems are two critical areas of a firm's operation that can affect profitability.

21. Do you keep records on the quality, service, price, and promptness of delivery of your sources of supply?

22. Have you analyzed the advantages and disadvantages of:

(a) Buying from several suppliers,

(b) Buying from a minimum number of suppliers?

23. Have you analyzed the advantages and disadvantages of buying through cooperatives or other systems?

24. Do you know:

(a) How long it usually takes to receive each order?

(b) How much inventory cushion (usually called safety stock) to have so you can maintain normal sales while you wait for the order to arrive?

25. Have you ever suffered because you were out of stock?

26. Do you know the optimum order quantity for each item you need?

27. Do you (or can you) take advantage of quantity discounts for large size single purchases?

28. Do you know your costs of ordering inventory and carrying inventory?

The more frequently you buy (smaller quantities per order), the higher your average ordering costs (clerical costs, postage, telephone costs etc.) will be, and the lower the average carrying costs (storage, loss through pilferage, obsolescence, etc.) will be. On the other hand, the larger the quantity per order, the lower the average ordering cost and the higher the carrying costs. A balance should be struck so that the minimum cost overall for ordering and carrying inventory can be achieved.

29. Do you keep records of inventory for each item?

These records should be kept current by making entries whenever items are added to or removed from inventory. Simple records on 3 x 5 or 5 x 7 cards can be used with each item being listed on a separate card. Proper records will show for each item: quantity in stock, quantity on order, date of order, slow or fast seller, and valuations (which are important for taxes and your own analyses.)

Other Financial Records

30. Do you have an accounts payable ledger?

This ledger will show what, whom, and why you owe. Such records should help you make your payments on schedule. Any expense not paid on time could adversely affect your credit, but even more importantly such records should help you take advantage of discounts which can help boost your profits.

31. Do you have an accounts receivable ledger?

This ledger will show who owes money to your firm. It shows how much is owed, how long it has been outstanding and why the money is owed. Overdue accounts could indicate that your credit granting policy needs to be reviewed and that you may not be getting the cash into the firm quickly enough to pay your own bills at the optimum time.

32. Do you have a cash receipts journal?

This journal records the cash received by source, day, and amount.

33. Do you have a cash payments journal?

This journal will be similar to the cash receipts journal but will show cash paid out instead of cash received. The two cash journals can be combined, if convenient.

34. Do you prepare an income (profit and loss or P&L) statement and a balance sheet?

These are statements about the condition of your firm at a specific time and show the income, expenses, assets, and liabilities of the firm. They are absolutely essential.

35. Do you prepare a budget?

You could think of a budget as a "record in advance," projecting "future" inflows and outflows for your business. A budget is usually prepared for a single year, generally to correspond with the accounting year. It is then, however broken down into quarterly and monthly projections.

There are different kinds of budget: cash, production, sales, etc. A cash budget, for example, will show the estimate of sales and expenses for a particular period of time. The cash budget forces the firm to think ahead by estimating its income and expenses. Once reasonable projections are made for every important product line or department, the owner-manager has set targets for employees to meet for sales and expenses. You must plan to assure a profit. And you must prepare a budget to plan.

10. Developing a Marketing Plan

Developing a marketing plan - marketing plan outline template, is a problem-solving document. Skilled problem solvers recognize that a big problem is usually the combination of several smaller problems. The best approach marketing planning is to solve each of the smaller problems first, thereby dividing the big problem into manageable pieces. Your marketing plan should take the same approach. It should be a guide on which to base decisions and should ensure that everyone in your organization is working together to achieve the same goals.

A good marketing plan can prevent your organization from reacting to problems in a piecemeal manner and even help in anticipating problems. Before your marketing plan can be developed, research must give you the basic guidelines: for whom you are designing your product or service (market segmentation), and exactly what that product or service should mean to those in the marketplace (market positioning). Below are some guidelines to help you develop a marketing plan to support the strategy you have selected for your organization.

Market Segmentation

Your sample marketing plan example - should recognize the various segments of the market for your product or service and indicate how to adjust your product to reach those distinct markets. Instead of marketing a product in one way to everyone, you must recognize that some segments are not only different, but better than others for your product. This approach can be helpful in penetrating markets that would be too broad and undefined without segmentation. No matter what you are making or selling, take the total market and divide it up like a pie chart. The divisions can be based on various criteria such as those listed below.

Demographics

This is the study of the distribution, density and vital statistics of a population, and includes such characteristics as

- Sex.
- Age.
- Education.
- Geographic location.
- Home ownership versus rental.
- Marital status.
- Size of family unit.
- Total income of family unit.
- Ethnic or religious background.
- Job classification blue collar versus salaried or professional.

Psycho-graphics

This is the study of how the human characteristics of consumers may have a bearing on their response to products, packaging, advertising and public relations efforts. Behavior may be measured as it involves an interplay among these broad sets of variables:

Predisposition - What is there about a person's past culture, heredity or upbringing that may influence his or her ability to consider purchasing one new product or service versus another?

Influences - What are the roles of social forces such as education, peer pressure or group acceptance in dictating a person's consumption patterns?

Product Attributes - What the product is or can be made to represent in the minds of consumers has a significant bearing on whether certain segments will accept the concept. These attributes may be suggested by the marketer or perceived by the customer. Some typical ways of describing a product include:

- **Price/value perception** - Is the item worth the price being asked?
- **Taste** - Does it have the right amount of sweetness or lightness?
- **Texture** - Does it have the accepted consistency or feel?
- **Quality** - What can be said about the quality of the ingredients or lack of artificial ingredients?
- **Benefits** - How does the consumer feel after using the product?
- **Trust** - Can the consumer rely on this particular brand? What about the reputation of the manufacturer in standing behind the product?

Life-Style

Statements consumers make about themselves through conspicuous consumption can be put to good use by research people who read the signals correctly. By studying behavioral variables, such as a person's use of time, services and products, researchers can identify some common factors that can predict future behavior.

Marketing Planning - Market Positioning

You must realize that your product or service cannot be all things to all people. Very few items on the market today have universal appeal. Even when dealing in basic commodities like table salt or aspirin, marketing people have gone to all sorts of extremes to create brand awareness and product differentiation. If your product or service is properly positioned, prospective purchasers or users should immediately recognize its unique benefits or advantages and be better able to assess it in comparison to your competition's offering. Positioning is how you give your product or service brand identification.

Positioning involves analyzing each market segment as defined by your research activities and developing a distinct position for each segment. Ask yourself how you want to appear to that segment, or what you must do for that segment to ensure that it buys your product or service. This will dictate different media and advertising appeals for each segment. For example, you may sell the same product in a range of packages or sizes, or make cosmetic changes in the product, producing private labels or selecting separate distribution channels to reach the various segments. Beer, for example, is sold on tap and in seven-ounce bottles, twelve-ounce cans and bottles, six-packs, twelve-packs, cases, and quart bottles and kegs of several sizes. The beer is the same but each package size may appeal to a separate market segment and have to be sold with a totally different appeal and through different retail outlets.

Remember that your marketing position can, and should, change to meet the current conditions of the market for your product. The ability of your company to adjust will be enhanced greatly by an up-to-date knowledge of the marketplace gained through continual monitoring. By having good data about your customers, the segments they fit into and the buying motives of those segments, you can select the position that makes the most sense.

While there are many possible marketing positions, most would fit into one of the following categories:

Positioning on specific product features - A very common approach, especially for industrial products. If your product or service has some unique features that have obvious value this may be the way to go.

Positioning on benefits - Strongly related to positioning on product features. Generally, this is more effective because you can talk to your customers about what your product or service can do for them. The features may be nice, but unless customers can be made to understand why the product will benefit them, you may not get the sale.

Positioning for a specific use - Related to benefit positioning. Consider Campbell's positioning of soups for cooking. An interesting extension is mood positioning: "Have a Coke and a smile." This works best when you can teach your customers how to use your product or when you use a promotional medium that allows a demonstration.

Positioning for user category - A few examples: "You've Come a Long Way Baby," "The Pepsi Generation" and "Breakfast of Champions." Be sure you show your product being used by models with whom your customers can identify.

Positioning against another product or a competing business - A strategy that ranges from implicit to explicit comparison. Implicit comparisons can be quite pointed; for example, Avis never mentions Hertz, but the message is clear. Explicit comparisons can take two major forms. The first form makes a comparison with a direct competitor and is aimed at attracting customers from the compared brand, which is usually the category leader. The second type does not attempt to attract the customers of the compared product, but rather uses the comparison as a reference point. Consider, for example, the positioning of the Volkswagen Dasher, which picks up speed faster than a Mercedes and has a bigger trunk than a Rolls Royce. This usually works to the advantage of the smaller business if you can capitalize on the tradition of cheering for the underdog. You can gain stature by comparing yourself to a larger competitor just as long as your customers remain convinced that you are trying harder.

Product class disassociation - A less common type of positioning. It is particularly effective when used to introduce a new product that differs from traditional products. Lead-free gasoline and tubeless tires were new product classes positioned against older products. Space-age technology may help you here. People have become accustomed to change and new products and are more willing to experiment than was true ten years ago. Even so, some people are more adventuresome and trusting than others and more apt to try a revolutionary product. The trick is to find out who are the potential brand switchers or experimenters and find out what it would take to get them to try your product. The obvious disadvantage of dealing with those who try new products is that they may move on to another brand just as easily. Brand loyalty is great as long as it is to your brand.

Hybrid bases - Incorporates elements from several types of positioning. Given the variety of possible bases for positioning, small business owners should consider the possibility of a hybrid approach. This is particularly true in smaller towns where there aren't enough customers in any segment to justify the expense of separate marketing approaches.

MARKETING PLAN WORKSHEET

This is the marketing plan of _____

I. MARKET ANALYSIS

A. Target Market - Who are the customers?

1. We will be selling primarily to (check all that apply):

Percent of Business

a. Private sector _____

b. Wholesalers _____

c. Retailers _____

d. Government _____

e. Other _____

2. We will be targeting customers by:

a. Product line/services. We will target specific lines
_____

b. Geographic area? Which areas? _____

c. Sales? We will target sales of _____

d. Industry? Our target industry is _____

e. Other? _____

3. How much will our selected market spend on our type of product or service this coming year?

_____

B. Competition

1. Who are our competitors?

Name _____

Address _____

Years in Business _____

Market Share _____

Price/Strategy _____

Product/Service _____

Features _____

Name _____

Address _____

Years in Business _____

Market Share _____

Price/Strategy _____

Product/Service _____

Features _____

2. How competitive is the market?

High _____

Medium _____

Low _____

3. List below your strengths and weaknesses compared to your competition (consider such areas as location, size of resources, reputation, services, personnel, etc.):

Strengths......Weaknesses

1._____ 1._____

2._____ 2._____

3._____ 3._____

4._____ 4._____

C. Environment

1. The following are some important economic factors that will affect our product or service (such as country growth, industry health, economic trends, taxes, rising energy prices, etc.):

_____

_____

_____

2. The following are some important legal factors that will affect our market:

_____

_____

_____

3. The following are some important government factors:

_____

_____

_____

4. The following are other environmental factors that will affect our market, but over which we have no control:

_____

_____

_____

II. Marketing Planning: PRODUCT OR SERVICE ANALYSIS

A. Description

1. Describe here what the product/service is and what it does:

_____

_____

_____

B. Comparison

1. What advantages does our product/service have over those of the competition (consider such things as unique features, patents, expertise, special training, etc.)?

_____

_____

_____

2. What disadvantages does it have?

_____

C. Some Considerations

1. Where will you get your materials and supplies?
_____

2. List other considerations:

_____

_____

III. MARKETING PLANING STRATEGIES - MARKET MIX

A. Image

1. First, what kind of image do we want to have (such as cheap but good, or exclusiveness, or customer-oriented or highest quality, or convenience, or speed, or ...)?

_____

B. Features

1. List the features we will emphasize:

a. _____

b. _____

c. _____

C. Pricing

1. We will be using the following pricing strategy:

a. Markup on cost _____ What % Markup? _____

b. Suggested price _____

c. Competitive _____

d. Below competition _____

e. Premium price _____

f. Other _____

2. Are our prices in line with our image?

YES ___ NO ___

3. Do our prices cover costs and leave a margin of profit?

YES ___ NO ___

D. Customer Services

1. List the customer services we provide:

a. _____

b. _____

c. _____

2. These are our sales/credit terms:

a. _____

b. _____

c. _____

3. The competition offers the following services:

a. _____

b. _____

c. _____

E. Advertising/Promotion

1. These are the things we wish to say about the business:

_____

2. We will use the following advertising/promotion sources:

1. Television _____

2. Radio _____

3. Direct mail _____

4. Personal contacts _____

5. Trade associations _____

6. Newspaper _____

7. Magazines _____

8. Yellow Pages _____

9. Billboard _____

10 Internet _____

11. Other _____ _____

3. The following are the reasons why we consider the media we have chosen to be the most effective:

_____

_____

11. Basics of Business Management

You are not ready to start your own business until you have given some thought to managing it. A business is an ongoing activity that doesn't run itself. As the manager you will have to set goals, determine how to reach those goals and make all the necessary decisions. You will have to purchase or make your product, price it, advertise it and sell it.

You will have to keep records, and determine costs. You will have to control inventory, make the right buying decisions and keep costs down. You will have to hire, train and motivate employees now or as you grow.

Setting Business Management Goals

Good small business management is the key to success and good management starts with setting goals. Set goals for yourself for the accomplishment of the many tasks necessary in starting and managing your business successfully. Be specific. Write down the goals in measurable terms of performance. Break major goals down into sub-goals, showing what you expect to achieve in the next two to three months, the next six months, the next year, and the next five years. Beside each goal and sub-goal place a specific date showing when it is to be achieved.

Plan the action you must take to attain the goals. While the effort required to reach each sub-goal should be great enough to challenge you, it should not be so great or unreasonable as to discourage you. Do not plan to reach too many goals all at one time. Establish priorities.

Plan in advance how to measure results so you can know exactly how well you are doing. This is what is meant by "measurable" goals. If you can't keep score as you go along you are likely to lose motivation. Re-work your plan of action to allow for obstacles which may stand in your way. Try to foresee obstacles and plan ways to avert or minimize them.

Buying

Skillful buying is an important essential of profitably managing a business. This is true whether you are a wholesaler or retailer of merchandise, a manufacturer or a service business operator. Some retailers say it is the most important single factor. Merchandise which is carefully purchased is easy to sell.

Determining what to buy means finding out the type, kind, quality, brand, size, color, style -whatever applies to your particular inventory - which will sell the best. This requires close attention to salespeople, trade journals, catalogs, and especially the likes and dislikes of your regular customers. Analyze your sales records. Even the manufacturer should view the problem through the eyes of customers before deciding what materials, parts, and supplies to purchase.

Know your regular customers, and make a good evaluation of the people you hope will become your customers. In what socioeconomic category are they? Are they homeowners or renters? Are they looking for price, style or quality? What is the predominant age category?

The age of your customers can be a prime consideration in establishing a purchasing pattern. Young people buy more frequently than most older people. They need more, have fewer responsibilities, and spend more on themselves. They are more conscious of style trends whether in wearing apparel, cars or electronic equipment. If you decide to cater to the young trade because they seem dominate in your area, your buying pattern will be completely different than if the more conservative middle-aged customers appear to be in the majority.

Study trade journals, newspaper advertisements, catalogs, window displays of businesses similar to yours. Ask advice of salespeople offering you merchandise, but buy sparingly from several suppliers rather than one, testing the water, so to speak, until you know what your best lines will be.

Locating suitable merchandise sources is not easy. You may buy directly from manufacturers or producers, from wholesalers, distributors or jobbers. Select the suppliers who sell what you need and can deliver it when you need it. (Distributors and jobbers are used by most business people for quick fill-ins between factory shipments.)

You may spread purchases among many suppliers to gain more favorable prices and promotional material. Or you may concentrate your purchases among a small number of suppliers to simplify your credit problems. This will also help you become known as the seller of a certain brand or line of merchandise, and to maintain a fixed standard in your products, if you are buying materials for manufacturing purposes.

When to buy is important if your business will have seasonal variations in sales volume. More stock will be needed prior to the seasonal upturn in sales volume. As sales decline, less merchandise is needed. This means purchases of goods for resale and materials for processing should vary accordingly.

At the outset, how much to buy is speculative. The best policy is to be frugal until you have had enough experience to judge your needs. On the other hand, you cannot sell merchandise if you do not have it.

To help solve buying problems, you should begin to keep stock control records at once. This will help you keep the stock in balance - neither too large nor too small - with a proper proportion and adequate assortment of products, sizes, colors, styles and qualities.

Fundamentally, there are two types of stock control - control in dollars and control in physical units. Dollar controls show the amount of money invested in each merchandise category. Unit controls indicate the number of individual items when and from whom purchased by category. A good stock control system can help you determine what, from whom, when, and how much to buy.

Pricing

Much of your success in manage a business will depend on how you price your services. If your prices are too low, you will not cover expenses; too high and you will lose sales volume. In both cases, you will not make a profit.

Before opening your business you must decide upon the general price level you expect to maintain. Will you cater to people buying in the high, medium, or low price range? Your choice of location, appearance of your establishment, quality of goods handled, and services to be offered will all depend on the customers you hope to attract, and so will your prices.

After establishing this general price level, you are ready to price individual items. In general, the price of an item must cover the cost of the item, all other costs, plus a profit. Thus, you will have to markup the item by a certain amount to cover costs and earn a profit. In a business that sells few items, total costs can easily be allocated to each item and a markup quickly determined. With a variety of items, allocating costs and determining markup may require an accountant. In retail operations, goods are often marked up by 50 to 100 percent or more just to earn a 5% to 10% profit!

Let us work through a markup example. Suppose your company sells one product, Product A. The supplier sells Product A to you for $5.00 each. You and your accountant determine the costs entailed in selling Product A are $4.00 per item, and you want a $1 per item profit. What is your markup? Well, the selling price is: $5 plus $4 plus $1 or $10; the markup therefore is $5. As a percentage, it is 100% ($5 markup = $5 cost of the item). So you have to markup Product A by 100% to make a 10% profit!

Many small business managers are interested in knowing what industry markup norms are for various products. Wholesalers, distributors, trade associations and business research companies publish a huge variety of such ratios and business statistics. They are useful as guidelines. Another ratio (in addition to the markup percentage) important to small firms is the Gross Margin Percentage (GMP).

The GMP is similar to your markup percentage but whereas markup refers to the percent above the cost to you of each item that you must set the selling price in order to cover all other costs and earn profits, the GMP shows the relationship between sales revenues minus the cost of the item, which is your gross margin, and your sales revenues. What the GMP is telling you is that your markup bears a certain relationship to your sales revenues. The markup percentage and the GMP are essentially the same formula, with the markup referring to individual item pricing and GMP referring to the item prices times the number of items sold (volume).

Perhaps an example will clarify the point. Your firm sells Product Z. It costs you $.70 each and you decide to sell it for $1 each to cover costs and profit. Your markup is 43%. Now let up say you sold 10,000 Product Z's Last month thus producing $10,000 in revenues. Your cost to purchase Product Z was $7000; your gross margin was $3,000 (revenues minus cost of goods sold). This is also your gross markup for the month's volume. Your GMP would be 30%. Both of these percentages use the same basic numbers, differing only in division. Both are used to establish a pricing system. And both are published and can be used as guidelines for small firms starting out. Often managers determine what Gross Margin Percentage they will need to earn a profit and simply go to a published Markup Table to find the percentage markup that correlates with that margin requirement.

While this discussion of pricing may appear, in some respects, to be directed only to the pricing of retail merchandise it can be applied to other types of businesses as well. For services the markup must cover selling and administrative costs in addition to the direct cost of performing a particular service. If you are manufacturing a product, the costs of direct labor, materials and supplies, parts purchased from other concerns, special tools and equipment, plant overhead, selling and administrative expenses must be carefully estimated. To compute a cost per unit requires an estimate of the number of units you plan to produce. Before your factory becomes too large it would be wise to consult an accountant about a cost accounting system.

Not all items are marked up by the average markup. Luxury articles will take more, staples less. For instance, increased sales volume from a lower-than-average markup on a certain item - a "loss leader" - may bring a higher gross profit unless the price is lowered too much. Then the resulting increase in sales will not raise the total gross profit enough to compensate for the low price.

Sometimes you may wish to sell a certain item or service at a lower markup in order to increase store traffic with the hope of increasing sales of regularly priced merchandise or generating a large number of new service contracts. Competitors' prices will also govern your prices. You cannot sell a product if your competitor is greatly underselling you. These and other reasons may cause you to vary your markup among items and services. There is no magic formula that will work on every product or every service all of the time. But you should keep in mind the overall average markup which you need to make a profit.

Selling

Whether you manage a factory, wholesale outlet, retail

store, service shop, or are a contractor, you will have to sell. No matter how good your product is, no matter what consumers think of it, you must sell to survive.

Direct selling methods are through personal sales efforts, advertising and, for many businesses, display - including the packaging and styling of the product itself - in windows, in the establishment, or both. Establishing a good reputation with the general public through courtesy and special services is an indirect method of selling. While the latter should never be neglected, this brief discussion will be confined to direct selling methods.

To establish your business on a firm footing requires a great deal of aggressive personal selling. You may have established competition to overcome. Or, if your idea is new with little or no competition, you have the extra problem of convincing people of the value of the new idea. Personal selling work is almost always necessary to accomplish this. If you are not a good salesperson, seek an employee or associate who is.

A second way to build sales is by advertising. This may be done through newspapers, shopping papers, the yellow pages section of the telephone directory, and other published periodicals; radio and television; handbills, and direct mail. The media you select, as well as the message and style of presentation, will depend upon the particular customers you wish to reach. Plan and prepare advertising carefully, or it will be ineffective. Most media will be able to describe the characteristics of their audience (readers, listeners, etc.). Since your initial planning described the characteristics of your potential customers, you want to match these characteristics with the media audience. If you are selling expensive jewelry, don't advertise in high school newspapers. If you repair bicycles, you probably should.

Advertising can be very expensive. It is wise to place a limit upon an amount to spend, then stay within that limit. To help you in determining how much to spend, study the operating ratios of similar businesses. Media advertising salespeople will help you plan and even prepare advertisements for you. Be sure to tell them your budget limitations.

A third method of stimulating sales is effective displays both in your place of business and outside it. If you have had no previous experience in display work, you will want to study the subject or turn the task over to someone else. Observe displays of other businesses and read books, trade magazines, and the literature supplied by equipment manufacturers. It may be wise to hire a display expert for your opening display and special events, or you may obtain the services of one on a part-time basis. Much depends on your type of business and what it requires.

The proper amount and types of selling effort to use vary from business to business and from owner to owner. Some businesses prosper with low-key sales efforts. Others, like the used-car lots, thrive on aggressive, hoop-la promotions.

In any event, the importance of effective selling cannot be over-emphasized.

On the other hand, don't lose sight of your major objective - to make a profit. Anyone can produce a large sales volume selling dollar bills for ninety cents. But that won't last long. So keep control of your costs, and price your product carefully.

Record Keeping

One essential element of business management is the keeping of adequate records. Study after study shows that many manager failures can be attributed to inadequate records or the owner's failure to use what information was available to him. Without records, the businessperson cannot see in advance which way the business is going. Up-to-date records may forecast impending disaster, forewarning you to take steps to avoid it. While extra work is required to keep an adequate set of records, you will be more than repaid for the effort and expense.

If you are not prepared to keep adequate records - or have someone keep them for you - you should not try to operate a small business. At a minimum, records are needed to substantiate:

1. Your returns under tax laws, including income tax and social security laws;

2. Your request for credit from equipment manufacturers

or a loan from a bank;

3. Your claims about the business, should you wish to sell it.

But most important, you need them to run your business successfully and to increase your profits. With an adequate. yet simple, bookkeeping system you can answer such questions as:

- How much business am I doing?
- What are my expenses? Which appear to be too high? What is my gross profit margin? My net profit?
- How much am I collecting on my charge business?
- What is the condition of my working capital?
- How much cash do I have on hand? How much in the bank? How much do I owe my suppliers?
- What is my net worth? That is, what is the value of my ownership of the business?
- What are the trends in my receipts, expenses, profits, and net worth? Is my financial position improving or growing worse? How do my assets compare with what I owe?
- What is the percentage of return on my investment?
- How many cents out of each dollar of sales are net profit?

Answer these and other questions by preparing and studying balance sheets and profit-and-loss statements. To do this, it is important that you record information about transactions as they occur. Keep this data in a detailed and orderly fashion and you will be able to answer the above questions. You will also have the answers to such other vital questions about your business as: What products or services do my customers like best? Next best? Not at all? Do I carry the merchandise most often requested? Am I qualified to render the services they demand most? How many of my charge customers are slow payers? Shall I switch to cash only, or use a credit card charge plan?

The kind of records and how many you need depends on your particular operation. A boy selling newspapers part time each day does not need inventory records. He buys and sells his entire stock each day. But shoe store or dress shop operators will soon find they cannot keep necessary inventory information in their heads.

Below is a list of records, grouped according to their use. No business will need them all. You may need only a few. As a matter of fact, you should not maintain a record without answering these three questions: (1) How will this record be used? (2) How important is the information likely to be? (3) Is the information available elsewhere in an equally accessible form?

The following list may call your attention to records you can use to great advantage:

- Inventory and Purchasing Records provide facts to help with buying and selling
- Inventory Control Record
- Item Perpetual Inventory Record
- Model Stock Plan

- Out-of-Stock Sheet
- Open-To-Buy Record
- Purchase Order File
- Open To Purchase Order File
- Supplier File
- Returned Goods File
- Price Change Book
- Accounts Payable Ledger
- Sales Records to help determine sales trends
- Individual Sales Transactions
- Summary of Daily Sales
- Sales Plan
- Sales Promotion Plan
- Cash Records to show what is happening to cash.
- Daily Cash Reconciliation
- Cash Receipts Journal
- Cash Disbursements Journal
- Bank Reconciliation
- Credit Records show who owes you money and whether they are paying on time.
- Charge Account Application
- Accounts Receivable Ledger
- Accounts Receivable Aging List
- Employee Records show legally required information and information helpful in the efficient management of personnel.
- Employee Earnings and Amounts Withheld
- Employees' Expense Allowances
- Employment Applications
- Record of Changes in Rate of Pay
- Record of Reasons for Termination of Employment Employee Benefits Record
- Job Descriptions
- Crucial Incidents Record

- Fixtures and Property Records list facts needed for taking depreciation allowances and for insurance coverage and claims.
- Equipment Record
- Insurance Register
- Bookkeeping Records, in addition to some of the above, are needed if you use a double-entry bookkeeping system.
- General Journal
- General Ledger

For efficient business operation, use information from records to keep inventory stock in line with sales, to watch trends, and for tax purposes. Use records to plan. A well thought-out business plan as a guide will strengthen your chances for success.

A record showing the data for your business plan is the budget. Work up a budget to help you determine just how much increase in profit is reasonably within your reach. The budget will answer such questions as: What sales will be needed to achieve my desired profit? What fixed expenses will be necessary to support these sales? What variable expenses will be incurred? A budget enables you to set a goal and determine what to do in order to reach it.

Compare your budget periodically with actual operations figures. With effective records you can do this. Then, where discrepancies show up you can take corrective action before it is too late. The right decisions for the right corrective action will depend upon your knowledge of management techniques in buying, pricing, selling, selecting and training personnel, and handling other management problems.

You probably are thinking you can hire a bookkeeper or an accountant to handle the record keeping for you. Yes, you can. But remember two very important facts:

1. Provide the accountant with accurate input. If you buy something and don't record the amount in your business checkbook, the accountant can't enter it. If you sell something for cash and don't record it, the accountant won't know about it. The records the accountant prepares will be no better than the information you provide.

2. Use the records to make decisions. If you went to a physician and he told you you were ill and needed certain medicine to get well, you would follow his advice. If you pay an accountant and he tells you your sales are down this year, don't hide your head in the sand and pretend the problem will go away. It won't.

Business Management Roll in Personnel Selection

If your business will be large enough to require outside help, an important responsibility will be the selection and training of one or more employees. You may start out with family members or business partners to help you. But if the business grows - as you hope it will - the time will come when you must select and train personnel.

Careful choice of personnel is essential. To select the right employees determine beforehand what you want each one to do.

Then look for applicants to fill these particular needs. In a small business you will need flexible employees who can shift from task to task as required. Include this in the description of the jobs you wish to fill. At the same time, look ahead and plan your hiring to assure an organization of individuals capable of performing every essential function. In a retail store, a salesperson may also do stock-keeping or bookkeeping at the outset, but as the business grows you will need sales people, stock-keepers and bookkeepers.

Once the job descriptions are written, line up applicants from whom to make a selection. Do not be swayed by customers who may suggest relatives. If the applicant does not succeed, you may lose a customer as well as an employee.

Some sources of possible new employees are:

1. Recommendations by friends, business acquaintances.

2. Employment agencies.

3. Placement bureaus of high schools, business schools, and colleges.

4. Trade and industrial associations.

5. Help-wanted ads in local newspapers.

Your next task is to screen want ad responses and/or application forms sent by employment agencies. Some applicants will be eliminated sight unseen. For each of the others, the application form or letter will serve as a basis for the interview which should be conducted in private. Put the applicant at ease by describing your business in general and the job in particular. Once you have done this, encourage the applicant to talk. Selecting the right person is extremely important. Ask your questions carefully to find out everything about the applicant that is pertinent to the job.

References are a must, and should be checked before making a final decision. Check through a personal visit or a phone call directly to the applicant's immediate former supervisor, if possible. Verify that the information given you is correct. Consider, with judgment, any negative comments you hear and what is not said.

Checking references can bring to light significant information which may save you money and future inconvenience.

Personnel Training

A well-selected employee is only a potential asset to your business. Whether or not he or she becomes a real asset depends upon your training. Remember:

- To allow sufficient time for training.
- Not to expect too much from the trainee in too short a time.
- To let the employee learn by performing under actual working conditions, with close supervision.
- To follow up on your training.

Check the employee's performance after he or she has been at work for a time. Re-explain key points and short cuts; bring the employee up to date on new developments and encourage questions. Training is a continuous process which becomes constructive supervision.

Personnel Supervision

Supervision is the third essential of personnel control. Good supervision will reduce the cost of operating your business by cutting down on the number of employee errors. If errors are corrected early, employees will get more satisfaction from their jobs and perform better.

Motivating Employees

Small businesses sometimes face special problems in motivating employees. In a large company, a good employee can see an opportunity to advance into management. In a small company, you are the management. One thing you may wish to consider is to give good employees a small share of the profits, either through part-ownership or a profit-sharing plan. Someone who has a "share of the action" is going to be more concerned about helping to make a success of the business.

12. Achieving Customer Satisfaction and Loyalty

Understanding and achieving Customer Satisfaction and Loyalty is essential for commercial success. This chapter explains how small companies can profit from understanding their customers.

Understanding one's customers is so important that large corporations spend hundreds of millions annually on market research. Although such formal research is important, a small firm can usually avoid this expense. Typically, the owner or manager of a small concern knows the customers personally. From this foundation, understanding of your customers can be built by a systematic effort. A comprehensive system for understanding is what Rudyard Kipling called his six honest serving men. "Their names are What and Why and When and How and Where and Who."

What

A seller characterizes what customers are buying as goods and services - toothpaste, drills, video games. cars. . . But understanding of buyers starts with the realization that they purchase benefits as well as products. Consumers don't select toothpaste. Instead. some will pay for a decay preventive. Some seek pleasant taste. Others want bright teeth. Or perhaps any formula at a bargain price will do.

Similarly, industrial purchasing agents are not really interested in drills. They want holes. They insist on quality appropriate for their purposes, reliable delivery when needed, safe operation, and reasonable prices.

Video games are fun. They are bought for home entertainment, family togetherness, development of personal dexterity, introduction to computers, among other satisfactions. Commercial customers include arcades, pizza parlors, and assorted enterprises. They benefit from a potential source of income, a means of attracting buyers to their premises, or perhaps a competitive move.

Similarly, cars are visible evidence of a person's wealth, reflection of life style, a private cabin for romance. Or they represent receipts from leases, means to pursue an occupation. . . Some people even buy cars for transportation.

You must find out, from their point of view, what customers are buying. The common names of products mean as little to them as the chemical names on the label of a proprietary drug. (A sick person's real need is safe. speedy relief.) Understanding your customers enables you to profit by providing what buyers seeks - satisfaction.

Products change, but basic benefits like personal hygiene, attractiveness, safety, entertainment, and privacy endure. So do commercial purposes such as quests for competitive superiority or profitability.

Successful manufacturers and service establishments produce benefits for which customers are willing to pay. Successful wholesalers and retailers select offerings of such demanded benefits that they can resell at a profit. Successful businesspeople, in other words. understand the reason for their customers' buying decisions

Why Customer Relationship Management

The reason that customers buy is logical from their point of view. Understanding customers derives from this fundamental premise. Don't argue with taste.

Everybody is unique. Each person has individual pressures and criteria. Moreover, perceptions differ. The astute businessperson deduces and accepts the buying logic of customers and serves them accordingly.

To learn why customers buy can be quite difficult.

Some buyers hide their true motivations. In many cases the reasons are obscure to the buyers themselves. Most purchase decisions are multi-causal. Often, conflicts abound. A car buyer may want the roominess of a large vehicle and the fuel economy of a subcompact. The resolution of such mutually exclusive desires is usually indeterminate.

Sometimes the reasons why customers buy are trivial. If

customers feel indifferent toward a product or store, the selection is apt to be happenstance. Perhaps several rival offerings meet all the conditions that a purchaser deems important. Consequently, minor factors govern. This explains the rationale of the consumer who chose a $ 22,000 car because its upholstery was most attractive. The point: Pay attention to details. They may be crucial to customers.

Often the best clues are the customers' actions. Shrewd businesspeople respect what people say, but pay special attention to what people do. More important than why customers buy is why former customers have taken their patronage elsewhere and why qualified buyers are not buying. What is now keeping them from buying?

Can this obstacle be surmounted? Businesspeople monitor competitive offerings and buyers' reactions to infer clues. Informal conversations may also reveal some reasons. Special offers may overcome resistance and boost profits.

All the time the manager must be careful to retain the company's regular customers. For instance, a specialty dress shop may try to widen its patronage through a new line at bargain prices. This move could disturb the store's usual patrons. They may take their trade to another store that caters exclusively to their social class.

Many of the dresses were bought for special occasions when projection of a genteel image was important to the customer. Understanding of customers includes awareness of the time of the purchase and use of the merchandise.

When

A seller must be ready when the buyer is, lest an opportunity be irretrievably lost. Customers buy when they want an offering and have the time and money to purchase it. Buying patterns can often be discerned from an analysis of customers and their purchases. For example, wants for many consumer goods and services are tied to customers' rites of passage. The following purchase occasions in the adult life cycle are typical:

1. Marriage, separation, divorce

2. Acquisition of a home

3. Change in employment or career

4. Graduate study; running for office

5. Health care, injury, illness

6. Pregnancy, nurture of children

7. Children enter school; graduate

8. Children leave home (for college or permanently)

9. Move to another area

10. Vacations; major social activities

11. Permanent retirement from work

12. Death of a family member.

Shrewd retailers keep track of such key buying events and gain a head start on making sales. Logs of birthdays and anniversaries are a case in point. Additional purchase occasions are impersonal. Seasonal factors include recurring holidays and weather changes. Among other favorable influences on purchases are start of the school year, semi-annual white sales, introduction of new models and clearance of old ones, special price concessions, and improvement in economic conditions or buyer's confidence.

Some of the latter factors also apply to manufacturers. Small plants work closely with their buyers' inventory managers and replenish stock at their reorder point. A current vogue is just-in-time delivery. Interactive computers make replenishment notices routine.

Many consumers have time for shopping only during off-hours. in the evenings, and on weekends. The trend from a single breadwinner per family toward having all adults of a household engage in commercial employment has intensified this time peculiarity. Astute retailers adjust their hours, staffing, and availability of merchandise to customers' shopping convenience. Bartenders know that business booms on payday. Manufacturers profit from timing their offers to their customers' budgetary cycles. Thus, knowing when products are bought and used is a valuable facet of understanding customers.

Although a transaction may be concluded in a moment, most purchases actually entail a drawn-out process.

This process will be described in the next section which analyzes how customers buy.

How

Knowledge of how customers buy pays off in several ways. (1) Sellers can design their offerings to meet the exact needs of their buyers. (2) Sellers can influence decision makers at crucial steps of the buying process. (3) Sellers can lay the groundwork for repeat business.

Buying methods are best visualized as processes. Household purchases usually start when a consumer has a desire or a problem that an acquisition might satisfy or solve. Industrial purchases usually start when a user or a routine sets off a signal (requisition) for approval of a procurement.

People are diverse. Every consumer, every firm pursues a buying process of its own. Buying processes also depend on the significance of the product to the buyer and on other circumstances. Although buying processes are not uniform. some steps are common to most of them. The seller needs to know only these critical steps when he or she can affect the outcome of the buying decision.

Shrewd sellers delve into the behavioral milestones of purchasers. But for each very important customer the buying process should be diagrammed individually, showing names of influencers at each decision stage, elapsed time between stages, and any other pertinent information.

Perhaps a change in life style or a demonstration at a friend's house has caused this consumer to recognize the need for a personal computer. But lack of knowledge and the fear of a wrong decision may counteract this desire. The process continues, however, if advertisements and expected benefits persuade the consumer to act. Despite budgetary constraints and uncertainty about future needs, the consumer proceeds to compare stores and brands.

At this search and evaluation stage advice from present satisfied customers is especially influential. Make sure your customers are satisfied and favorably recommend your merchandise or service. To the contrary, poor shopping facilities or irritating personnel can sway the potential customer against making the purchase from you.

Sooner or later, further search does not seem worthwhile. If the positives still outweigh the negatives, the consumer picks a store and brand. The transaction itself is consummated quickly, assuming the wanted item is available. The satisfied customer makes recommendations to others and gives you his or her repeated, regular business.

Businesspeople can create sales by predisposing potential buyers to their product or store. Manufacturers can offer exclusive benefits in their goods, such as friendly relations, efficient operations, and easy manuals. Enticing advertisements help persuade prospects to visit a retail outlet and ask about a particular brand. Creative salespeople overcome the customer's objections and doubts and close the sale. Post-transaction service keeps the customer satisfied. Referrals usually follow.

Specific details are needed to track acquisition of something complex, say a computer. On the other hand, less detail is needed if the purchase is laundry detergent or some other staple with which the customer is less involved. In the latter case, depletion of the home inventory triggers a routine, leading directly to choice: the usually purchased brand. If the usual brand is out-of-stock or another brand is on sale. a substitute may be bought quickly. Brand comparisons follow or may be omitted.

Some products are bought when an emergency need for them arises. A physical examination and the filling of a prescription are urgent when sickness strikes. Arrangements for funerals follow immediately after the death of a family member. Umbrellas are in demand when it rains. An unexpected snow storm generates extra calls for tire chains, towing services, and car batteries. Often, convenient availability determines when these goods and services are purchased. And even if customers do have ample time to select merchandise, sellers who stand ready to supply wanted or expected brands are apt to gain preference and profit when shoppers decide where to buy.

People want options. Although convenient availability is the main buying criterion for many routine household products, savvy merchants stock a selection conforming to the diverse preferences of their patrons. Some people demand manufacturers' advertised brands. Resellers' brands are favored by others. On some classes of goods, generic brands have become popular in recent years. Moreover, many consumers seek occasional variety. Clearly the decision of which products to stock is important.

It is more important yet on shopping goods because buyers compare them before purchase. And it is most important on specialty goods, those preselected by brand name. If a store does not stock these uniquely wanted brands, a prospect will leave without buying. Whoever offers them on acceptable terms gains the sale.

Where

From a multitude of studies emerge different criteria for deciding where to shop. Most research on the subject agrees that store location is a major consideration, Stores usually draw most of their patronage from their surrounding neighborhood.

Savvy store managers make a special effort to understand the shopping-related motivations and preferences of local residents. New managers of fast-food units, for example, canvass nearby dwellings and introduce themselves to the households. Some supermarkets maintain consumer advisory boards to elicit suggestions and reactions. Other means of communication with customers include informal conversations at the store and suggestion boxes with interviews and awards.

Incidentally, complaints are an excellent guide for making store policies more amenable to customers. Personnel should be instructed to thank patrons for their comments. Prompt consideration, followed by a personal letter from the store manager, is highly desirable.

Location is extremely important to "captive" buyers. Exclusively franchised utilities, shops in isolated hotels. and cafeterias or automatic vending machines in factories are examples. At the opposite extreme, shoppers escape spatial restrictions by buying from mail-order firms or telephone solicitors.

Other patronage influences vary. They depend on the type of product. type of store, and the characteristics of the consumer. The offered assortment's perceived quality. depth, and breadth certainly are very important. along with price, This does not imply that all goods have to be top quality or all prices the lowest. Perceptions are decisive.

If quality seems high, some customers infer that prices are high too regardless of the facts. The important point is to understand customers and to provide what causes them to buy. For example, assurance of repair service weighs heavily with the worrier type of customer. A convenience-minded buyer is concerned with parking space or delivery service.

Of course, shoppers must be told that wanted goods and services are available. Advertising helps disseminate this information. So does a store's reputation for consistent policies of satisfying its customers.

Occasional promotions inject some excitement into the tedium of shopping. Some clients like to socialize, which can absorb much of an employee's time and may even annoy other buyers. Nevertheless, personnel should be friendly and helpful. Also influential, for some customers, is the apparent socio-economic level of other shoppers.

Personal affinity for other customers or for salespeople is a decisive factor in the success of party-selling, e.g., household goods and in-home selling (cosmetics). The choice of where to buy items requiring major outlays (securities, and insurance) often revolves around from whom to buy.

In selecting a retail store, many customers consider physical features. Layouts can invite or repel patronage. Motorists who are in a hurry, for instance, are apt to use a gasoline station at which business can be transacted quickly. Altogether, buyers perceive a mix of tangible and intangible factors that comprise a store's atmosphere. Accordingly, they either do or don't feel comfortable about shopping there.

To the casual observer, all supermarkets seem more or Hess alike, But. in fact, store managers can regulate many of the above-mentioned variables and thereby affect where shoppers buy. According to recent studies in several American cities, household buyers perceive supermarkets in their neighborhood as sufficiently different to determine their patronage preference. The four main types of supermarkets offer: (1) High quality at commensurate prices, (2) Lowest price level in the area, (3) Swift completion, (4) Friendly atmosphere. Each can profit by appealing to a different segment of buyers. the topic of the next section.

Who

Identification of customers and prospects makes effective targeting possible. Small business owners pride themselves on knowing their customers personally. In the industrial field, understanding of each major customer and buying influence is essential. When dealing with a large number of customers, however, individual familiarity is not feasible. Hence mass merchandisers and others in this situation group their customers, whose reactions to offerings are similar, into segments. Then they design a separate appropriate marketing program for each segment.

Strategies vary, A small firm might prosper by concentrating its resources on one segment. Because customers are volatile, the specializing firm is vulnerable to sudden change in its target segment's patronage. Hence some companies address several segments simultaneously. Although expensive, a strategy of employing different tactics for different segments can be quite profitable. Other firms scatter offers to just anybody. They hope that segments will select themselves.

One basis for segmentation is geographic. Retail customers are apt to live or work in the store's vicinity. Industrial buyers tend to concentrate regionally. So do users of services. Intensive cultivation of local potential customers can be efficient and lucrative. Personal knowledge of local buyers and a shared community spirit help cement relations with these customers.

Segmentation is an art. All "honest serving men" - what, why, when, how, where, as well as who - can be the key to segmentation. Whatever the basis, each identified segment should have sufficient purchasing power to make a special effort commercially worthwhile. Accessibility is vital. How can the segment be reached? Are advertisements, telephone solicitations, or personal visits efficient? How about trade shows or personal contacts? The ideal segment is stable in purchase needs and loyalty, helping you fend off competition.

Besides segmentation, understanding of customers also requires insight into their buying roles. The buyer for a one-person household or one-person business is the initiator of the order, the decider, and the user. Even in this case, however, some outsiders are influential.

In larger households or businesses, these buying roles are usually played by separate individuals. It helps you to know who activates (requisitions) purchases, who exerts influence, who decides what and where to buy, who uses the product-and what their criteria are. Then you tailor and target your offerings to satisfy each major participant in the buying process.

As has been shown, understanding of customers enables a seller to increase sales. This same understanding can equally serve to reduce costs. Higher sales at lower costs inevitably boost profits.

A small firm that understands its customers can buy or produce exactly what they want-and nothing else. The firm's sales effort is efficient because it builds on why its customers want to buy not on why others buy, or why the vendor wants to sell.

Merchandise can be ready when customers need it. Thus a knowledgeable seller avoids unnecessary inventory costs or penalties for late delivery. Understanding how customers buy lets a seller employ promotional media, appeals, and timing for maximum effectiveness. Transportation costs are lowered by shipping merchandise to where it is needed. Knowledge of who comprises suitable segments and the separate buying roles can reduce the waste of soliciting unqualified or uninterested people.

Customers Are Dynamic

The best source for you to learn about customers is your personal interaction with them. At work, social and civic activities, and chance encounters, people talk and reveal their attitudes and motivation. Listen to your customers. You can also keep abreast of purchasing patterns by observing competitors' practices and by asking sales personnel who is buying what, where.

Articles in business and trade newspapers and magazines give information on products, trends, marketing, finance, the economy. Trade directories, Yellow Pages, and brokers' direct-mail lists identify who buyers are, and most industries have associations and specialized marketing research that provide insights for understanding customers.

13. Five Special Free Bonuses (download links are provided)

a. Excel Financial Projections Creator - simply type in your business' details and assumptions and it will automatically produce a comprehensive set of financial projections for your specific business, including: Start-Up Expenses, Projected Balance Sheet, Projected Cash Flow Statement, Financial Ratios Analysis, Projected Profit and Loss Statement, Break Even Analysis, and many more.

Copy the following link to your browser and save the file to your PC:

http://www.bizmove.com/bp/projections.xlsx

a1. Detailed guide that will walk you step by step and show you exactly how to effectively use the above Excel Financial Projections Creator.

Copy the following link to your browser and save the file to your PC:

http://www.bizmove.com/bp/projections-guide.doc

b. Simple business plan template in MS Word format - allows you to craft a good business plan quickly and easily.

Copy the following link to your browser and save the file to your PC:

http://www.bizmove.com/tools/bptemplate.docx

c. How to Improve Your Leadership and Management Skills (eBook) - Discover powerful strategies to motivate and inspire your people to bring out the best in them. Be the boss people want to give 200 percent for.

Copy the following link to your browser and save the file to your PC:

http://www.bizmove.com/bp/leadership.pdf

d. Video Training Course: How To Gain A Competitive Advantage

Learn how to get a competitive advantage with this course. Learn how to brand, study your competition, identify customers and their preferences, create pricing strategies and much more. Leverage the uniqueness of your business to create a real competitive advantage.

Copy the following link to your browser to access the online course.:

http://www.bizmove.com/business-training/how-to-gain-a-competitive-advantage.htm

e. Video Training Course: How To Grow Your Business

You have started your business and now you think you are ready to grow. How do you really know if you and your company are ready for the next step? This course will help you determine if a growth opportunity is right for you.

Copy the following link to your browser to access the online course.:

http://www.bizmove.com/business-training/how-to-grow-an-established-company.htm

Made in the USA
Lexington, KY
15 September 2018